Norse Spirituality

Unlocking Norse Paganism, Shamanism, Magic, Asatru, Elder Futhark Runes, Divination, Spells, and Heathenry

© Copyright 2023 - All rights reserved.

The content contained within this book may not be reproduced, duplicated, or transmitted without direct written permission from the author or the publisher.

Under no circumstances will any blame or legal responsibility be held against the publisher, or author, for any damages, reparation, or monetary loss due to the information contained within this book, either directly or indirectly.

Legal Notice:

This book is copyright protected. It is only for personal use. You cannot amend, distribute, sell, use, quote, or paraphrase any part, or the content within this book, without the consent of the author or publisher.

Disclaimer Notice:

Please note the information contained within this document is for educational and entertainment purposes only. All effort has been executed to present accurate, up-to-date, reliable, and complete information. No warranties of any kind are declared or implied. Readers acknowledge that the author is not engaging in the rendering of legal, financial, medical, or professional advice. The content within this book has been derived from various sources. Please consult a licensed professional before attempting any techniques outlined in this book.

By reading this document, the reader agrees that under no circumstances is the author responsible for any losses, direct or indirect, that are incurred as a result of the use of the information contained within this document, including, but not limited to, errors, omissions, or inaccuracies.

Free Bonus from Silvia Hill available for limited time

Hi Spirituality Lovers!

My name is Silvia Hill, and first off, I want to THANK YOU for reading my book.

Now you have a chance to join my exclusive spirituality email list so you can get the ebooks below for free as well as the potential to get more spirituality ebooks for free! Simply click the link below to join.

P.S. Remember that it's 100% free to join the list.

~~$27~~ FREE BONUSES

- 9 Types of Spirit Guides and How to Connect to Them
- How to Develop Your Intuition: 7 Secrets for Psychic Development and Tarot Reading
- Tarot Reading Secrets for Love, Career, and General Messages

Access your free bonuses here
https://livetolearn.lpages.co/norse-spirituality-paperback/

Table of Contents

INTRODUCTION 1
CHAPTER 1: THE OLD NORSE RELIGION 3
CHAPTER 2: PANTHEON AND COSMOLOGY 13
CHAPTER 3: DEATH AND THE AFTERLIFE 22
CHAPTER 4: ASATRU VS. HEATHENRY 30
CHAPTER 5: SEIÐR MAGIC AND SHAMANISM 39
CHAPTER 6: WORKING WITH THE GODDESS FREYJA 47
CHAPTER 7: JOURNEYING THROUGH YGGDRASILL 55
CHAPTER 8: NORSE RUNES 101 64
CHAPTER 9: RUNIC DIVINATION AND MAGIC 80
CHAPTER 10: GALDR MAGIC 89
CONCLUSION 97
GLOSSARY: NORSE TERMS 99
HERE'S ANOTHER BOOK BY SILVIA HILL THAT YOU
MIGHT LIKE 106
FREE BONUS FROM SILVIA HILL AVAILABLE FOR LIMITED
TIME 107
REFERENCES 108

Introduction

Norse spirituality is a religious endeavor built on Scandinavian beliefs and practices that predate Christianity. Norse paganism and spirituality date back to the Iron Age's Germanic peoples. However, these spiritual beliefs never stopped expanding and evolving until Christianity swept the lands of Scandinavia.

Most kings were pressured into converting at the start of Christianization because of economic and political reasons. While some people converted, others didn't like the idea of having to choose one spiritual path over another. This is why they decided to worship the Christian god and incorporate him into their polytheistic pantheon. This was one of the main reasons why Norse religious practices never withered away with time. Since the Norse found a way to amalgamate both religious systems, numerous Pagan rituals, lore, and myths were significantly influenced by Christianity. The opposite is also true.

Even today, many practitioners of Norse spirituality like to explore their own take on the practice. This is partly because many ancient Norse religions didn't leave written records of their practices; most of their teachings were orally transmitted, which is why there isn't a holy book you can refer to for instructions. Most of what we know comes from archaeological evidence that gives us insight into ancient Norse folklore, myths, deities, and religious practices. Roman sources and Old Norse manuscripts, created post-Christianization, also provides clues about their teachings. Snorri Sturluson's Prose Edda, the Poetic

Edda, and the Hávamál are a few examples of these records.

Norse religion is a huge umbrella that encompasses many paths and branches you can follow. Some of these paths are community-based, while others rely on solitary practices. This is why you must consider your preferences and community when choosing a path. Even though some religious paths allow you to adopt the religion as a philosophy or adapt it to your lifestyle and the dynamics of modern life, others require you to follow the traditions exactly as they are.

Studying each of these branches in-depth would be impossible before deciding which path to follow. Fortunately, this book is the perfect place to start. Here, you will learn everything you need to know about Norse spirituality. This book serves as the ultimate guide to Norse Paganism, Shamanism, Magic, Asatru, Elder Futhark Runes, Divination, Spells, and Heathenry.

Upon reading this guide, you'll learn each belief system's origins and how it differs from other paths. You'll also understand the key practices of each belief system and come across step-by-step instructions on practical spiritual techniques that you can try out. The last few chapters delve deep into Norse runes, runic divination and magic, and Galdr magic, and offer hands-on methods to use runes and incorporate them into meditative practices, cast runic spells and charms, and conduct the High-Seat Rite.

This book is perfect for beginners and more advanced practitioners alike, as it is easy to read and contains both knowledge and practical instructions.

Chapter 1: The Old Norse Religion

The Norse are one of the most mysterious ancient civilizations in the world. The origins of their religion and mythology have often been debated since no literature existed from the Norsemen themselves prior to the Christianization of Scandinavia. Most elements in Norse mythology can be traced through Indo-European and Germanic parallels, showing that their religion had a polytheistic structure, including a pantheon of gods and goddesses similar to how other religions perceived deities.

The Norse are one of the most mysterious ancient civilizations in the world.
https://www.pexels.com/photo/wooden-runes-and-stones-scattered-on-wool-plaid-6739035/

Norse mythology is a complex and intricate system of beliefs that spans several centuries. It includes stories about the world's creation, gods and goddesses, humans, giants, and other creatures. The myths are often narrated in poetry to make them easier to remember by people who did not have access to written records at that time.

Norse mythology is an integral part of the Viking Age, being a source of inspiration for many people during that period. Their stories are still widely known today, and many myths have been adapted into other forms of media, including movies and video games.

If historians were to summarize the Old Norse Religion, they'd say that the religion of the ancient Norse people was polytheistic. Their deities were split into two groups, Æsir and Vanir. In some sources, these groups were portrayed as initially having been at war with one another until both sides realized that they each had the power to destroy the other (but not without destroying themselves in the process). The two most well-known gods in the Norse pantheon were Odin and Thor. According to Norse mythology, other races besides humans, such as dwarves, giants, and elves, inhabited this world. The Norse view of the universe is based on Yggdrasil, a mythical tree with branches spreading to all parts of the cosmos.

This polytheistic religion is complex and includes elements of shamanism, animism, and ancestor worship. Norse mythology is a rich and varied body of tales and includes stories about gods, goddesses, heroes, and villains. The myths are often told through poetry and songs. Also, Norse gods have many different roles in their stories; they can be benevolent and cruel or kind and vindictive. In some tales, they take human form to interact with mortals, while other stories portray them as living apart from humans in faraway lands. This chapter is a brief introduction to Norse mythology and religion. It expands on the origin of the Old Norse Religion and beliefs. Despite being forgotten during the Christianization of Scandinavia, it remains one of the most popular religions in the world.

Origin

The origin of the Norse religion is a complex one. It developed during the Iron Age when the Norsemen settled in Scandinavia and began interacting with their neighbors. As they did so, they started to adopt elements of their neighbors' religions. The Vikings were among the last people in Europe to convert to Christianity, and this process was not peaceful. The religion we know as Norse mythology today results from centuries of interaction between different cultures and religions. It is believed that the Norse people adopted many of their gods from the Germanic tribes living in Scandinavia then.

Iron Age

The earliest evidence of Norse religion comes from the Iron Age. Archaeologists have found numerous artifacts that suggest the existence of a religion. The Norse worldview was a development of earlier Germanic religions. Many motifs associated with the sun, including wheel crosses and imagery associated with solar worship, appeared in Iron Age Scandinavia. The Vikings held beliefs in spirits and magic, which are now thought to have been abandoned by the people of Scandinavia during the fifth century B.C., only to be revived centuries later when Viking culture came into prominence. The Germanic languages developed over several hundred years, starting about 1,000 B.C.E in what is now Denmark and spreading to neighboring lands as well. The archaeologist Gabriel Turville-Petre, among others, has suggested that early Scandinavian accounts by Tacitus offer some valuable insights into later Norse religious practices. Tacitus describes the Germanic peoples as having priests who officiated at sacred sites. He also notes that they have a hierarchical structure involving seasonal sacrifices and feasts.

Viking Age Expansion

Vikings, the people of Scandinavia, left their home countries and settled in other parts of Northwestern Europe. The populations of some areas, like Iceland and the Orkney and Shetland Islands in Scotland, were relatively low. The Viking settlers greatly influenced the Scandinavian religious beliefs of people living in Iceland. When Norwegian settlers arrived, they brought with them their god Thor, the most popular deity among them. According to some saga accounts, Freyr was also worshipped by some of the settlers.

Odin's role in Icelandic society was less prominent than it was elsewhere. Unlike other Nordic countries, Iceland lacked a royal family or central government to enforce religious adherence. Instead, multiple communities had differing beliefs from the time of its first settlement. In the late ninth century, Scandinavian settlers brought their religion to Britain. The English church felt the need to convert the population that had immigrated with Old Norse names referencing ancient religious entities such as alfr and skratii (elves and demons).

Decline Due to Christianization

By the time Christianity reached Scandinavia, it had already been established as a major religion in Europe. While a wealth of sources documents the Christianization of Scandinavia, historians have had difficulty understanding this process because few narratives describe how Scandinavian society was converted.

When Christian missionaries from the British Isles traveled to northern Europe in the eighth century, King Charlemagne encouraged them to bring their religion and its accompanying culture and customs to his own people in Denmark. King Horik altered the religious practices of his country when he came into power.

During his visit to England, King Hákon the Good of Norway converted to Christianity. Upon his return to Norway, he encouraged Christian priests to preach among the population. However, this angered some members of the pagan community, who burned three churches in Trondheim to protest what they saw as an unwanted foreign influence. Norwegian resistance to Christianity continued under his successor Harald Greycloak. Under pressure from the Danish king, Haakon Sigurdsson agreed to be baptized and allowed Christians to preach in Norway. Although Christianization had progressed steadily throughout Norway during Haakon's reign, he continued to support pagan sacrificial customs and asserted the superiority of traditional deities. During this era, the Norsemen's native pagan beliefs were transformed into a unique combination of Christian and pre-Christian practices.

After the death of Haakon in 995, Olaf Tryggvason took over. He was determined to convert members of the Norwegian upper classes. He destroyed shrines and killed those he believed to be sorcerers. When and how Sweden became Christian is unclear, but by the early 11th century, at least its kings had converted—and a few decades later, it seems that every Swede was also part of the Church.

Conversion to Christianity provided the upper classes and kings with support from Christian rulers in the form of capital, goods, and military support. Even though mass conversions became the norm, the Christian missionaries found it challenging to convince religious Norse followers to accept Christianity. As mentioned, the Norse religion is polytheistic and revolves around worshiping several gods and goddesses. The followers of the Norse religion simply absorbed Jesus as another God into their faith. Christianity inspired new forms of pagan expressions, such as by influencing various myths. Because of their relative isolation, Scandinavians living in rural areas may have held onto certain pre-Christian beliefs for longer than those living in cities.

Post-Christianization Survival

Although paganism had ceased to threaten Christianity by the 12th century seriously, Scandinavian priests continued to oppose it.

The stories of the Norse gods and goddesses were passed down orally for at least two centuries before being written down in the 13th century. It is unclear how these stories were passed down to later generations. Some historians theorize that some pagans may have held onto their belief system during the 11th and 12th centuries. For example, some scholars believe that the old gods were worshipped secretly by individuals who were hesitant to abandon their pagan past. However, this theory has little evidence beyond a few myths about hidden witches and sorcerers.

The mythological themes of Old Norse poetry continued to be a source of inspiration for poets in the eleventh century when King Cnut ruled England. Saxo studied the ancient practices of his ancestors, not in an attempt to revive them but because he was interested in their history.

Snorri reexamined the myths passed down through generations, writing about them from a cultural historian's perspective. As a result, Norse mythology remained popular for hundreds of years after belief in its gods had faded away. Despite the prevalence of Christianity in Scandinavia during this period, pagan rituals were observed for centuries afterward. Today, Norse mythology is still important to many people and is a source of inspiration in art, literature, and music.

Beliefs

The ancient Norse religion was polytheistic and focused on worshipping a pantheon of gods, goddesses, and other supernatural beings. The religion was practiced by people living in Scandinavia, Iceland, the Faroe Islands, and parts of Britain and Ireland.

Deities

The Old Norse religion was centered on a pantheon of various deities. Some of the most notable deities in this ancient religion included Odin, the god of war and wisdom; Freyja, goddess of love and fertility; Thor, the god of thunder; and Loki, the trickster god. From roughly 400 – 1,000 AD, these gods were worshipped by communities throughout Northern Europe. Many aspects of Old Norse beliefs can still be seen today, such as the prominence of natural elements like fire and water in rituals and prayers. Even though much about religion has been lost over time, it remains a fascinating subject for historians today. Thanks to curiosity and modern research into these early beliefs, we can gain a deeper understanding of this rich spiritual tradition that was so important to our ancestors.

The deities of the Norse pantheon can be divided into two main groups, The Aesir, which is associated with order and justice, and the Vanir, which is associated with fertility and nature. The difference between these two groups can be seen in their respective attitudes toward humanity. The Aesir were said to be more remote and reserved, while the Vanir were said to be more approachable and interested in human affairs.

1. Aesir

The Aesir are a group of deities representing the principle of order in the universe; this group includes some of the most well-known gods and goddesses of Norse mythology, such as Odin, Thor, and Freyja. These powerful beings governed the different aspects of human life, such as war, weather, home, fertility, and health. They were believed to live in Asgard, a mythical realm that was said to be connected to our world by the rainbow bridge called Bifrost. Despite their power, many of the Aesir were not seen as wholly good or wholly evil. Instead, they were believed to engage in a constant struggle for supremacy over the realms and over humanity itself. For this reason, people during this time often turned to seers and diviners for guidance on how best to gain the gods' favor. Though the religion of the Aesir eventually died out, it left behind a rich legacy of mythology that continues to fascinate us today.

2. Vanir

The Old Norse religion was centered on a complex network of gods and goddesses, known collectively as the Vanir. The Vanir were associated with nature and fertility and played a crucial role in Norse mythology. Some of the most well-known figures from this pantheon include Njord, Freyr, Freyja, and Skadi. Each of these deities had its powers and areas of influence, but together, they formed a more extensive spiritual system deeply rooted in animism and mysticism. Despite its decline during the Christianization of Scandinavia, this ancient belief system had a lasting impact on Nordic culture, influencing everything from art and architecture to mythology and folklore. Today, many modern practitioners have embraced the Vanir as ancestors or guides in their spiritual journeys. Ultimately, the strength and resilience of this enduring faith are a testament to its timelessness and power.

Odin

The Norse pantheon was home to an array of powerful and complex gods believed to have played a crucial role in shaping the landscape and events of the world. One of the most significant figures in this pantheon was Odin, a powerful god who was represented as a mysterious bearded man wielding a spear. He was associated with many critical aspects of life and death, from wisdom and war to poetry and magic. He was said to have created the first humans from two trees and welcomed dead warriors into the warriors' heaven, Valhalla. In many ways, Odin embodied all that the ancient Norse people valued. His great power made him an object of reverence and fear, but he also had great kindness when it came to those who honored him properly. Ultimately, his wisdom made him the most influential member of the Norse pantheon.

Ragnarök

Ragnarök, or the twilight of the gods, is a significant event in Norse mythology that has captured the imagination of people all over the world. The story goes that an epic battle will occur between the gods and their enemies, ultimately destroying all things. However, many believe that Ragnarök may be more than just a myth. Some scholars have speculated that it represents an ecological cataclysm brought about by humanity's damaging impact on the natural world. Others see it as a metaphor for our impending death or a coming cultural shift. Regardless of what Ragnarök may signify, one thing is clear, this compelling story has inspired generations of people with its vivid imagery and vast implications. It is truly an enduring legend, both mysterious and inspiring.

Afterlife

In Norse mythology, the afterlife was known as the realm of Helheim. This was not considered a place of punishment or suffering, but instead, a place where souls would be reunited with loved ones and spend eternity in peace. According to legend, Helheim was ruled over by the goddess Hel, who had control over all mortal souls that made their way there. She would grant each soul whatever level of joy or bliss it craved for eternity, making no distinction between those who had lived noble lives and those who had been cruel or wicked during their time on Earth. Thus, contrary to popular belief, life after death in Norse mythology was not a grim fate but rather a reward for a well-lived life. Indeed, many ancient Norse believed that choosing their path in life and taking responsibility for their actions could ultimately lead to immortality in Helheim.

The World Tree

The World Tree is a central concept in Norse Paganism, representing the connection between earth and sky. According to Norse myths, the branches of this massive tree reach up into the heavens while its roots grow deep into the earth, connecting these seemingly disparate realms. Not only does this image represent a profound sense of connection between all beings and all things, but it also underscores the importance of balance and harmony in nature. After all, if one side of the tree were to outgrow or overpower the other, it could result in chaos and imbalance. By embodying these ideals, the World Tree reminds us that we must always strive to maintain balance in our lives and our broader interactions with the world around us.

Asgard

Norse Paganism is centered on the idea of Asgard, a realm that is home to the gods of the Norse pantheon. According to ancient Norse belief, Asgard was located at the top of the world tree Yggdrasil, serving as a sort of paradise for these deities. Although comparatively small, Asgard held everything its inhabitants could need or want - fertile fields, forests full of game, rivers teeming with fish, and even mountains made of precious metals. At the center of this wondrous world lay Aesir Hall, a soaring structure built entirely out of gold and topped with a towering dome. For many years, Norse Pagans worshipped their gods in this majestic setting, drawing strength and inspiration from the splendor and grandeur of Asgard. Today, while few people still formally practice Norse Paganism, many still look upon examples like Asgard as sources of beauty and wonder that we can all strive to emulate in our own lives.

Midgard

According to ancient Norse tradition, Midgard is a vast plane containing everything from towering mountains and deep lakes to sprawling forests and wild plains. Within this eternal landscape lives an incredible array of creatures, from mighty gods and noble giants to fierce dragons and cunning trolls. To truly understand the world of Midgard is to understand that everything in it is united by a web of relationships that moves in cycles of constant change and transformation.

Norse Paganism Now

Norse Paganism is a spiritual tradition rooted in pre-Christian Northern Europe. Today, many people worldwide still practice it to connect with their ancestors and honor the cycles of life, death, and rebirth. Whether as a spiritual practice or simply for fun cultural enrichment, Norse Paganism is living proof that ancient traditions are still alive in our modern world.

Throughout history, countless belief systems and spiritual traditions have helped shape the world we live in today, and many people around the globe still practice Norse Paganism. At its core, this ancient spiritual practice is based on the cycles of life, death, and rebirth found in all aspects of nature. By honoring and connecting with their ancestors through ritual, teachings, and communal gatherings, adherents of Norse Paganism gain a deeper understanding and appreciation of these transcendent cycles.

Whether participating in traditional ceremonies or simply taking time each day to connect with Nature as a whole, these individuals understand that we must honor the past if we wish to preserve the future. So, while Norse Paganism might seem like a foreign concept to some people, it is an essential part of our shared history and one that continues to have a profound impact on us all.

Chapter 2: Pantheon and Cosmology

Ancient cultures didn't have the science or technology that we have today. To make sense of the world around them and their place in it, each ancient culture came up with its own cosmology theory. Norse cosmology is about the study and understanding of the cosmos. It is a fascinating topic that includes concepts like the Nine Worlds, the creation myth, how the Norse people believe the world will end, and the tree of life. Scholars owe so much to literary works like the Poetic and Prose Edda by Snorri Sturluson as it gave them a clear idea of how the Norse people perceived the universe.

Pantheon Roman Temple in Rome.
https://www.pexels.com/photo/pantheon-roman-temple-in-rome-2928046/

Norse cosmology is similar to the shamanic traditions in other European and Asian cultures. Yet, it succeeded in standing out and having its own identity. Many Of its concepts are based in the otherworld – the realm of the spirits. This realm is usually invisible to the living. However, in some tales, both worlds overlapped with one another. One of the main concepts in Norse cosmology is Yggdrasill which was one of the most significant trees for the Norse people. They had an interesting view of the world, seeing it as a large disc with the mighty tree of life, Yggdrasill, standing at its center. The Norse people believed that the world was divided into nine realms. From the branches of the Yggdrasill rises each of these nine realms.

Yggdrasill (The Tree of Life)

As mentioned, the Yggdrasill has branches holding all nine realms. This tree exists in all worlds: the underworld, the physical world, and the heavens. The Poetic Edda describes Yggdrasill as an ash tree with three roots, and according to the poem, three wells provide these roots with water. Völuspá, a poem from the Poetic Edda, mentions the Urda or Urdarbrunnr, one of the three wells located in the sky. Three maidens tend to this well. These maidens are the gods of fate and are called Norn. Verdandi is the Norn of the present, Urda is the Norn of the past, and Skuld is the Norn of the future. These three maidens are responsible for the destiny of all beings. The whole universe depends on this tree; the world will fall apart without it. Hvergelmir, the second of the three wells, lies under the second root, which stretches to Niflheim, one of the Nine Worlds. The third root belongs to the counselor of the gods, Mimir, who is known for his wisdom. This root stretches out to Jotunheim, the realm of the giants. In fact, in the Poetic Edda, Yggdrasill was sometimes referred to as Mímameiðr, which means "post of Mimir." This indicates that the tree and the third well may be connected to Mimir. One day, when Ragnarok (the end of the world) arrives, the tree will tremble as a warning that the end is here.

The branches of Yggdrasill stretch out over the whole world while the roots stretch throughout different realms. The first root stretches to Midgard (the physical realm), the second root stretches to Utgard (the realm of the giants), and the third root stretches to Hel (the underworld). The name Yggdrasill is believed to mean "Horse of

Odin." The first part of the name, "Yggr," means terrible, which is one of Odin's many names, and the second part, "drasil," means horse. Odin is the main god in Norse mythology and will be discussed later in the chapter. Although the name Terrible isn't pleasant, it signifies Odin's power and how people were terrified of him. The tree's name is meant to honor Odin.

In the poem Völuspá, Yggdrasill is described as the sky's friend, and above the clouds lies its crown. Hávamál, another poem from the Poetic Edda, states that winds always blow around the tree. The Norse people believed that only the shamans could see the trees' roots before they died. They also believed that Yggdrasill was the sacred place where all the gods held their meetings. Various mythical creatures live near or around the tree. Duneyrr, Dainn, Dvalin, and Durathror are the four stags that eat the leaves of the Yggdrasill.

A dragon named Nidhogg lives around the base of the tree and feeds off its second root. On the branches stands an eagle whose name is unknown, and snakes are living near its roots. All these animals feed on Yggdrasill. However, the tree is never impacted, nor will it ever wither. It is strong and will last for as long as the universe lasts.

No one knows who created Yggdrasill, as it existed well before the universe or mankind came to be. It stood alone with the void before time itself. The nine realms were created around its roots when the universe was created.

The Nine Realms

The Nine worlds spread out from the branches of Yggdrasill, which also connects these worlds together. Unfortunately, Poetic Edda and other literary works don't mention the locations of these worlds or provide clear information or descriptions of some of them. The Nine realms were originally called:

- **Midgard:** The physical world where mankind exists.
- **Asgard:** The world where Aesir (a family of Norse gods) exists.
- **Vanaheim:** The world where Vanir (another race of gods that were known for their magic) exists.

- **Alfheim:** The realm where the Bright Elves live.
- **Svartalfheim:** The world of the Black Elves.
- **Jotunheim:** The world of the Giants.
- **Muspelheim/Muspell:** The realm of chaos.
- **Niflheim:** The world of mist and ice.
- **Nidavellir:** The world of the dwarves.

When Snorri wrote the Poetic Edda, he changed the names of some of the realms, merged a couple of them together, and added a new realm.

- **Midgard:** This one remains the physical world, but according to the Poetic Edda, it exists between Jotunheim and Asgard.
- **Asgard:** The Aesir Gods still reside in Asgard and are connected to the physical world (Midgard) by a rainbow bridge referred to as Bifrost.
- **Vanaheim:** Remains the world of the Vanir
- **Alfheim:** It became the realm of all the Elves
- **Svartalfheim/Nidavellir:** These are the two realms that were merged together and have become the world of the dwarves that exist beneath the earth.
- **Jotunheim:** The world of the Frost Giants and the Giants
- **Muspelheim:** This became the realm of a giant made of fire called Surt and his forces of chaos. It also became the realm of fire.
- **Niflheim:** The world of mist, ice, and now, snow as well. It also exists near Muspelheim.
- **Hel:** This is the realm that Snorri added, and it is the realm of the afterlife where the spirits of the dead live on.

Now let's take a more detailed look into each of the nine realms.

Midgard

Midgard is the realm of mankind. Ask and Embla were the first two people to ever exist in this world. Similar to Adam and Eve, all mankind descended from them. When Odin and his brothers Ve and Vili first created the first man and woman, they realized that these new creatures weren't as mighty as the gods or as strong as the giants. They couldn't live among giants as they would easily devour them, so they needed protection.

For this reason, Odin created Midgard so mankind could live, prosper, and be safe. The Prose Edda described Midgard as circular and surrounded by a deep sea, and on the coasts of the sea, some giants were given lands by Odin and his brothers. However, the gods later built a wall around this circular round world to protect its new beings from the giants. The wall was made using the eyelashes of the giant Ymir.

Asgard

After they created mankind, the gods created Asgard, surrounding it with high walls to protect it. Before Snorri wrote the Poetic Edda, it was believed that Asgard was part of Midgard. However, his poems made it clear that Asgard is located in the heavens. The Bifrost Bridge connects Asgard with Midgard.

. Odin and the rest of the Aesir (family of gods) lived in Asgard. A peace treaty between the Aesir and the Vanir allowed some Vanir deities to live in Asgard. Some of the most famous Aesir gods that lived on Asgard are names that you may already be familiar with, thanks to the Thor movies like Odin, Thor, and Loki. Asgard is a heavenly place with many towers standing tall. Odin's throne exists in a place called Valhalla, which is also a part of Asgard. Odin can see the whole universe from Hildskjalf. However, it isn't clear if Hlidskjalf is an object or a place.

Vanaheim

Vanir, another race of Norse gods, lived in Vanaheim. They were fertility gods who practiced magic. Just like how some of the Vanir live on Asgard, there are also Aesirs that live in Vanaheim as well. The Poetic Edda never gave any details of what Vanaheim looked like. However, magic and fertility were the main themes that defined this realm. It is believed to be a beautiful realm filled with light and magic.

Alfheim

Alfheim is another heavenly realm, and it is located near Asgard. It is the home of the elves, who are enchanted beings. They are very beautiful creatures who are creative and known for their love of music and art. Similar to Vanaheim, there is no accurate description of

Alfheim in any works of literature. However, since it is the realm of the elves, it is believed to be as beautiful as these creatures.

Svartalfheim/Nidavellir

Svartalfheim/Nidavellir is located below Midgard. It is the realm where the dwarves lived, which is very different from the bright and lovely Alfheim. It is a dark place filled with smoke from the fire torches placed over its walls.

Jotunheim

This is the realm where Frost Giants and the giants reside. It is located in an interesting position near the two main realms, Asgard and Midgard.

There is a river separating Asgard from Jotunheim called Ifing. This realm, also called Utgard, is known for being a wild and chaotic place where magic is practiced freely with no rules governing it. The famous god Loki (on which the Marvel character is based) was born in Jotunheim. Like his movie character, Loki was the god of mischief and was famous for playing tricks on the gods. He is the reflection of the place he came from. Jotunheim was a dangerous place, so many gods preferred to stay away from it. However, some legends mentioned that there were gods who traveled to Jotunheim from time to time.

Muspelheim

According to the Poetic Edda, Muspelheim played a significant role in the creation of the universe. Surtr, the fire giant, lives in the realm of fire. It is believed that Surtr will be the one who destroys the universe, including Asgard, during Ragnarok. It is also known as one of the oldest of the nine realms.

Niflheim

Niflheim is considered older than all the other nine realms. This realm of snow and ice is where the universe was born. Niflheim is the coldest realm, so cold that no living being, deity, or giant can live in it.

Hel

This realm shares a close connection with the trickster god Loki since his daughter Hel is its ruler.

This realm is very gloomy and dark since it is located underneath Yggdrasill's roots. Odin was wary that Loki's children might cause trouble just like their father. He sent each of them to a faraway realm, and Hel was sent to one of the darkest realms. The realm has a massive wall that surrounds it. There is just one gate to this realm. However, it isn't easily accessible. It takes a long and arduous journey that involves crossing one of the most dangerous rivers in the nine realms. This realm later became the realm of the dead. However, only the spirits of the people who died of natural causes like old age and disease are allowed to travel there. It isn't mentioned in any literary work how or why Hel became a realm of the dead.

The Norse Gods and Goddesses

In Norse mythology, there are only two races of gods, The Vanir and the Aesir. The Aesir race includes some of the most well-known gods in Norse mythology, and there is much known about them, unlike the Vanir race, about whom knowledge is limited to their realm and some of their deities like Njörðr who had two children, Freyja and Freyr. Njörðr and his children lived in Asgard. They first arrived as hostages but remained there to maintain the peace between the two races. They lived there in peace, were respected by all the deities in Asgard, and learned to work and co-exist together.

Let's take a look at the most prominent gods and goddesses from both races.

Odin

Odin is the supreme god and the most significant deity in Norse mythology. He is the king of Asgard and is often referred to as the Allfather or the father of the gods. Thor movies showed Odin exactly as he was depicted in Norse mythology, an old, bearded man with one eye. Highly respected by all the other deities, no other deity is as strong or as powerful as Odin. He is the god of war and death and is known for his knowledge and wisdom. Odin is very wise and has a thirst for knowledge. He even sacrificed his eye to gain more wisdom and enlightenment and reveal the universe's many secrets. This supreme deity is also the god of poets and has immense knowledge of the runes, which will be discussed later in the book.

Thor

For many people, thanks to the Marvel movies, Thor needs no introduction. The movies made him the most popular and interesting

Norse deity. In Norse mythology, he is equally fascinating. Like in the movies, Thor is Odin's son, the god of thunder, and he wields his famous and mighty hammer, Mjölnir. In some cases, Mjölnir could also bring the dead back to life. He is the strongest Norse god, which is why he is also the protector of Asgard. Thor is responsible for lighting, storms, and rain. Similar to how he is portrayed in the movies, Thor is big and strong but has a red beard and red hair.

Another thing the movies got right was that Thor is a real hero, more so than Odin and Loki, who are more occupied with scheming. He is fierce and courageous and never shies away from battle or from facing a dangerous beast. In fact, Thor enjoys fighting. Besides his hammer, Thor also has a magical belt called Megingjörd. As a result of Thor's power and many other attributes, most of the Vikings revered and worshiped him.

Loki

Another popular deity, thanks to Marvel movies, is Loki. However, Loki is exceptionally different from the movies; he never became the heroic character the movies made him out to be. Loki isn't Odin's adopted son or Thor's brother. He is often referred to as Odin's brother, but not biologically; they are more like blood brothers. Loki was a trickster god of mischief. He can shape-shift into any creature of any gender, and he often uses this ability to play tricks on the other gods to cause chaos. However, every once in a while, he helps the other gods. He is so witty that it's safe to say wit and trickery are his only weapons since he never carried a real one. Although Loki is never described as evil, he was behind some terrible events in Norse mythology, like orchestrating the murder of Odin's son Balder.

Freya

Unlike all the gods mentioned so far, Freya belongs to the Vanir race. She is known for her immense power since she is the goddess of fate and war. Freya also has a tender side being the deity of beauty and love.

She is the ruler of Fólkvangr, which is a heavenly place where half the spirits of the people who died in battle traveled. The other half went to Valhalla. Similar to her people, Freya is known for her magical abilities and has the power to influence people's destinies. In fact, she has the gift of prophecy, which she uses to defeat her enemies and help her friends. Freya has a magical cloak that gives her the ability to fly.

Norse mythology is fascinating with its several deities, worlds, and how the people viewed the world. However, it isn't just the world of the living that is filled with stories and excitement. The mythology of death and the afterlife is equally fascinating, about which you will find out more in the next chapter.

Chapter 3: Death and the Afterlife

Vikings were known for being some of the fiercest warriors at the time. They believed that there was nothing more honorable than dying in battle. Dying in battle was their way into Valhalla, the Viking's equivalent to heaven. For this reason, they fought courageously and fearlessly in the hopes of reaching it after death.

In every religion or set of beliefs, people have their own idea of the soul and what happens to it after death.
https://www.pexels.com/photo/table-setting-with-lighted-candles-and-flowers-7705408/

This chapter will focus on the Norse people's beliefs about the soul, death, and the afterlife.

The Concept of the Soul in Norse Religion

In every religion or set of beliefs, people have their own idea of the soul and what happens to it after death. Norse mythology is no different. People often see themselves as having two parts, the body and the spirit. The Norse people, on the other hand, had a different view of the soul. The word soul in the old Norse language is *sál*. However, before Christianity, this word didn't exist. It only came to be when Norse people began to convert to Christianity. This shows that they didn't even have the concept of a soul before Christianity. What we call the soul, the Norse people called the self.

The self wasn't one single thing but something much more complicated. The concept of the self in Norse mythology isn't similar to how Christians or other religions view the soul or the afterlife, whether now or during ancient times. They didn't see the soul/self as just one thing but as consisting of various parts that don't necessarily correspond with one another. You won't find any of these parts familiar or similar to anything represented in Christianity.

The Norse people believed that four elements make up each person's soul/self.

Fylgja

Fylgja is pronounced as "filg-ya," emphasizing the first part, meaning "follower." The plural of the word is "fylgjur," and it is pronounced as "filg-yur." In Norse mythology, Fylgja was a spirit that mirrored one's personality and had the gift of second sight. The person and their Fylgja were very much connected and often had similar characteristics. For instance, a brave soldier's Fylgja could be a lion, while a quiet person's Fylgja could be a deer, and in very rare cases, some people could have a human as their Fylgja. Think of it like the Patronus from Harry Potter, which is linked to a person's personality and can look like an animal or any other creature that reflects their key traits.

Hamr

This word is pronounced like "hammer," meaning "skin." This element represents a person's physical appearance. The eyes can see the physical appearance since what the eyes see is usually real and fixed in reality. However, in Norse mythology, not everything the senses perceived was necessarily real. The Norse people believed that their appearance changed after death. The Hamr changed after death by either changing color or shape-shifting.

Hamingja

This word is pronounced like "*hahm-ing-ya*" with emphasis on the first syllable and represents "luck." However, the Norse people had a different view of the concept of luck than how it is perceived nowadays. Luck was just like honesty, courage, and a sense of humor, and it was a quality that a person developed or inherited from their family. Luck was what made a person powerful, wealthy, and successful. In fact, the Norse people regarded luck as a separate entity from the other four elements of the self/soul. A person's Hamingja might come back during reincarnation, which means it didn't always stay with them in the afterlife. Hamingja was passed down by family members to their descendants, especially if the newborn and the dead family member shared the same name. According to the Viga-Glums Saga, the Hamingja could choose the descendant it would pass itself down to, even if they didn't share the same name with their ancestor. A person could also lend a friend or a loved one their Hamingja during their lifetime if they felt they could use some luck.

Hugr

The word "Hugr" means "mind." It represents the personality or characteristics that a person acquired when they were alive. It is similar to the concept of the inner self. The Hugr stayed with a person even after death, which means that a person's thoughts, feelings, qualities, and everything that made them who they were when they were alive remained intact in the afterlife.

The Norse people believed that where one ended up in the afterlife differed depending on the person. One person could live on as a ghost haunting their home, remain in their grave for eternity, or reside in any heavenly realm with the deities. There were many possibilities. However, in some cases, not all the elements of a person's soul end up in the same place in the afterlife. Similar to modern and ancient cultures, the Norse people believed in the concept of reincarnation and that a part of the soul could be reborn, leaving the rest behind.

Reincarnation

Reincarnation is the idea that after a person dies, their soul is reborn and begins a new life cycle in a different body.

The Norse people believed in the concept of reincarnation. This was evident in how they believed that the Hamingja or Hugr would pass down to newborns from dead relatives. This means they believed that the soul, or at least a part of it, could come back after rebirth. Unlike in other beliefs, the gods in Norse mythology didn't judge the soul based on how good or bad the person's actions were when they were alive. The gods chose who ended up in their realm. It was either for personal gains, like in the case of Odin, or based on how a person died. What the person did while alive never factored in the gods' or Valkyries' choice. Since there was no punishment or reward, the idea that the Norse people believed that the soul could come back through rebirth seems plausible.

The Afterlife

The Norse people believed in the afterlife. They believed that the spirit of the dead would go to the otherworld, a spiritual realm. There were five realms that the Norse people believed the spirits ended up in after death. Here, we will look at these five realms and the meaning behind each one.

Valhalla

It means "the hall of the fallen," which was located in Asgard. Although the Poetic Edda mentions that Valhalla was in Asgard, there are other parts in the poem that suggest that it might be in the underworld. It was a heavenly place where the souls of the departed spent the afterlife. However, not all souls ended up there. Odin was the one who chose the souls that he found worthy of this honor. Valhalla is a place fit for heroic warriors. Grímnismál, from the poetic Edda, shows that Valhalla was built with weapons and gold. In each corner, there are feasting tables with plenty of food surrounded by the most comfortable seats.

Fierce wolves were standing by the gates, and eagles were flying above to guard them.

It is clear from Valhalla's description that it was a place like no other. It's no wonder every Viking warrior dreamed of dying in battle as they knew the luxurious life awaiting them. However, the Viking didn't spend all day resting and eating. During the day, they fought like warriors. Naturally, they got hurt and wounded, but they were completely healed in the evening. They got rewarded after a long day of fighting with delicious meals and an endless supply of the finest drinks. Odin chose the spirits' of these warriors for a reason. When Ragnarok (the end of the world) arrives, Odin will need a brave army by his side. However, according to legends, Odin and his army will meet their demise.

The Prose Edda details how the souls entered Valhalla. The souls of dead warriors who died in battle were the only ones allowed entry to Valhalla. Odin and the Valkyries chose these souls, but the reason was obvious: he wanted fierce soldiers for the end-of-the-world battle who would spend their time training and preparing for Ragnarok. Valhalla was the home of rulers, warriors, and heroes. If a person wasn't a warrior or didn't die in battle, then they would end up in a different realm.

Hel

Hel is a word from the Old Norse language that means "Hidden." This was another place where some spirits of the dead ended up, symbolizing the underworld. Loki's daughter Hel was the ruler of this realm. Since this was similar to the underworld, Hel is believed to exist beneath the earth. However, other sources state that Hel was located in the realm of Niflheim. It shares some similarities with the Greek underworld, one being that a gigantic dog also guarded it. Although Hel and Hell have similar spellings, the Norse underworld and the Christian Hell don't share any similarities.

Unlike Valhalla, literary works haven't provided enough descriptions of Hel to give us an idea of what it might look like. However, it was often discussed using a positive tone and terms when it was mentioned. It was a place where all the spirits of the dead, except warriors, were allowed to spend the afterlife. Hel was different from the concepts of heaven and hell that most people are familiar with. In other words, Hel was neither a reward like heaven nor a place for torment like hell. It was simply a place where people continued to live their lives after death.

However, the Prose Edda portrayed Hel in a different light from all the other literary sources. Snorri wrote the Poetic and Prose Edda after the arrival of Christianity, so he might have been influenced by the Christian concept of Hell. However, there aren't many scholars who agree with Snorri's portrayal. In his Prose and Poetic Edda, he stated that only people who died from natural causes like old age and disease are allowed to enter Hel.

The Realm of Rán

Rán was a goddess and a giantess who ruled over this realm. She was married to the Lord of the sea, Aegir, who was also a giant. The Realm of Rán was located at the bottom of the sea. The souls of the people who drowned at sea ended up in this realm. Her husband Aegir is often portrayed in a positive light, but the same can't be said of Rán. She would capture sailors with her net to take their treasures and drown them. Their souls spend the afterlife in her realm. In fact, her realm shone brightly as a result of all the treasure she took and kept there.

Folkvangr

The word Folkvangr means "the field of people" It was another afterlife realm located in Asgard and ruled by the Vanir goddess Freya. The Grímnismál from the Poetic Edda speaks of an agreement between Odin and Freya where they both split the souls of the fallen warriors, Odin took half, and they went to Valhalla, and Freya took the other half and went to Folkvangr. Judging from the meaning behind its name, it is also believed that Folkvangr was a palace for the souls of all people, not just soldiers. This was mentioned in another literary source, Egil's Saga. However, another translation of the name "the field of the army" could suggest that this was a realm like Valhalla that only accepted *dead warriors*. Not much is known about what this realm was like. However, Freya was known as one of the kindest goddesses in Norse mythology. She was a fair and generous ruler, and her realm reflected her true character.

The Burial Mound

In some cases, the soul didn't end up in any of these realms as it remained in the grave or wherever the body was buried. This was referred to as "the burial mound." Some souls didn't stay in the burial mound as they would walk among the living to haunt them and cause trouble.

The Norse Rites and Rituals in Funerals

Since the Vikings believed in the afterlife, naturally, they would prepare their dead for the journey. Some certain traditions and rituals were associated with their funerals. They would either cremate or bury their deceased. Early Vikings preferred cremation as a method to send their dead to the afterlife. They were followers of paganism and believed that the smoke would help the soul cross to the afterlife. The remains were placed in an urn, similar to what people do nowadays. A person must be buried with their belongings. However, they should be personal and specific items that reflect who they were and what they did when they were alive. For instance, a painter was buried with their painting equipment, a warrior was buried with their weapons, and wealthy women were buried with their jewelry. The dead in Norse mythology continued their lives in one form or another in the afterlife, so it made sense that they were buried with their personal belongings.

Some Vikings would bury the body or the cremated remains of their dead. They would either bury them in burial mounds, grave fields, or shallow graves. If you watch any movie or TV show about the Vikings, you will notice that boats were often featured in their funerals. Boats were significant in Norse mythology. They represented the safe journey a person took to the afterlife. The Vikings built burial mounds that took the shape of ships to guarantee that the deceased would travel safely to the afterlife. These ship-shaped graves were only meant for the wealthy. However, unlike what pop culture might make you believe, Vikings sending out boats to the sea with deceased bodies and burning them occurred on rare occasions. The boats at the time cost a lot to make, so setting these boats on fire every time someone died wasn't a viable option.

The Vikings dressed their dead in new clothes. They prepared specific clothing items for burials and funerals. It was important that the deceased enter the afterlife in new clothes to honor this occasion. During the funeral, they would chant, sing, and serve alcohol and food. The mourners would bring valuable gifts like jewelry or weapons that were then burned or buried with the deceased.

Ancestor Worship

Norse people highly revered their ancestors. Before Christianity, ancestor worship was a massive part of pagans' and Norse cultures' beliefs. Whether it was old or modern pagans, they all held their ancestors in very high regard. The ancestors were the spirits of the dead that the living kept in their memories. Their descendants honored and revered them hoping to get their blessings. The living never forgot their dead, no matter how long ago they had passed. One of their main blessings was the *hamingja*, a female guardian spirit that the ancestors bestowed upon their descendants.

Modern pagans, similar to the Vikings, still highly revere their ancestors and believe they can bless them.

In Norse mythology, death wasn't the end of the soul's journey; it was merely the beginning. The soul continued living in various ways, whether by living in any realm of the dead or coming back through reincarnation. Interestingly, living an honorable life didn't factor into how one would spend their afterlife; how one died made the difference. An honorable death in a battle was what secured them an entrance to Valhalla, where the souls spent their lives in the realm of the gods. The afterlife was a very significant concept in Norse mythology, which was evident by how they prepared their dead for the journey and how they were concerned about dying honorably.

Chapter 4: Asatru vs. Heathenry

Like most ancient traditions and religions, the beliefs of the Vikings and what we know as Norse mythology are dense and intricate. And, like most remnants of ancient cultures, it has been up for reinterpretation by contemporary practitioners who have found poignant elements that feel relevant to the present. Within this context, there has been a great deal of talk regarding heathenism and Asatru, two branches of Norse mythology and spirituality that have found a new audience. This chapter explores each practice in depth – its origins, historical background, and how it can be interpreted for modern life.

Thunder's hammer, the Irminsul, and the Woden's knot.
https://commons.wikimedia.org/wiki/File:Heathen_symbols.svg

Heathenism

On the surface, heathenism seems straightforward, but that's because anyone with a Judeo-Christian background will likely take the word for it to mean something else entirely. Others would easily conflate heathenism with paganism, even though they are very different concepts. Broadly speaking, both terms can be applied to anyone who does not follow the Abrahamic, monotheistic line of faith, with paganism encompassing a wide variety of indigenous and polytheistic religions worldwide. Heathenism is a catchall term to encompass anyone who does not identify themselves as a believer in monotheistic religions at large but who also follows the dictates of Anglo-Saxon spirituality and makes it their business to understand its roots in Norse mythology. To further illustrate the point, heathenry is part of Germanic polytheism, combining modern traditions with ancient Iceland beliefs. This entails the Anglo-Saxons, the Franks, and generally any ancient group that spoke German and its variants. The traditions of the Scots, while somewhat related, do not really come into play here. It's really all about codifying and celebrating the way of the Vikings.

Influences

Nowadays, when someone calls themselves a heathen, people tend to think of it in the derogatory, heavily Christian sense in that an individual does not believe in god or the prophets. The term has been widely used as a way to verbally bludgeon non-believers and ostracize them. If heathens could choose any other term to describe themselves, they maybe would. Unfortunately, the term came about due to a shortage of native words to help describe the myriad number of polytheistic religious beliefs and practices that were so popular in certain parts of the Western world before the advent of Christianity. "Heathen" is actually Old Norse for "heiðinn" and meant the "Old Way," signifying an attempt to hold onto the ancient traditions and beliefs of yore.

True heathens who wear the label proudly devote a great deal of time and energy brushing up on various texts detailing aspects of historical belief and practice. To really understand heathenism, one must also work to understand the origins and development of the tradition and how it came to be in its contemporary form. It is deeply influenced by Old Norse and Anglo-Saxon poetry, Icelandic sagas, early German literature, and even complex medieval legal codes and material as recent as 19th-century folkloric collections, some of which have anonymous sources. In fact, academic studies on archaeology and history also serve as critical primary texts for practitioners, which reflects a continuous attempt to better understand ancient traditions and ensure their practical application in the modern day.

Books, Books, and More Books

To better understand the origins and historical background of heathenism, it helps to turn to literature. The written word forms the backbone for much of the practice and how heathens form their own worldview. For the novice, reading could be a much more accessible and copacetic way of learning about the religion instead of getting involved in a local chapter right away!

One classic text that practitioners find to be inspiring is Padraic Colum's 1920 mythological tome, "Children of Odin." The illustrations are pure eye candy, but this book is primarily noted for how well it outlines important Viking myths and Norse spirituality. It's also an excellent example of how the work of more contemporary authors, practitioners, and historians has helped to influence a new generation of heathens by making these ancient stories more accessible.

Most people will tell you never to forget the medievalists since they arguably did the most work to collate all of the different practices, literary traditions, and stories, even as Christianity grew widespread in Western Europe and threatened to eradicate this important culture. Snorri Sturluson wrote Edda around 1220, which is an earlier attempt to compile Norse mythology. While this is considered an essential text, it is also known to be somewhat flawed since most writers working to interpret these traditions and stories often did so for a wider Christian audience, so there are vagaries here or there that can irritate more well-versed heathens. However, despite the loose interpretation of important cultural markers for the Vikings, the text is still an essential primer of religious beliefs and practices prevalent in pagan times.

Of course, poetry plays a significant role in heathenism and is a good way of getting more information regarding the ancients' cultural context, beliefs, and rites. One work that is considered to be a foundational text is Poetic Edda, a wonderfully rich poem that delves into the mythology and heroic poems of Iceland, drawing inspiration from a manuscript dating to 1270. The poems are intricate and magical, describing ancient gods and goddesses, the Valkyries, dwarves and dragons, and so on. There is something for everyone, and while it's definitely not for the newbie, it is an excellent way for those hoping to understand heathenism better to begin familiarizing themselves with its history.

Rites and Practices

In terms of their beliefs, heathens believe in the ancient Norse gods and uphold their important place within their religion. Heathens try very hard to uphold the rites and practices of the ancients while making them easier to blend into everyday contemporary life.

In terms of major celebrations, heathens hold feasts around what they call blots and occasions, such as weddings, baby-naming, or seasonal holidays like All Hollow's Eve. They also perform rites to honor different gods and goddesses or when they need to ask them for help.

Traditionally, a blot was a ritual sacrifice of an animal to the gods, which was then followed by a feast in which the meat was shared among the participants. A modern version of a blot still focuses on eating and drinking and paying homage to the gods. However, the ritualistic sacrifice of an animal isn't on the menu these days, and it's fine to have one indoors without having a major festival outdoors. Although, if one is to be had outdoors, heathens throw in a few choice items into a fire to pay respects to the gods and bring good fortune to themselves and their community.

A *symbel* is different in that eating is pulled out of the equation, and a ritual drinking ceremony is performed instead. Typically, the drink will be imbibed from a drinking horn, just as the ancient Vikings used to do, although finding an appropriate chalice is a viable option. Mead is the drink of choice, but wine could also work for most occasions. In a symbel ceremony, heathens could pass the horn around to all participating so that the drink is blessed and enough merry toasts are made to the gods, ancestors, and so on. A drink offering may also be made to the gods by pouring out the contents in their honor.

Beyond these major celebratory occasions, heathens like to make offerings to the ancients in everyday life to pay tribute to them. Heathens believe that there are "hidden folk" in the home, such as elves or garden gnomes, so leaving a bowl of cake or a pint of ale is seen as a kind gesture. These offerings tend to be left at a small altar in the garden that the heathen has made explicitly for this purpose.

Asatru

Asatru is a slightly different take on the ancient traditions than heathenism, but they are often confused with one another. One key difference is that Asatru represents more modern influences, reviving pre-Christian Germanic polytheistic religions while emphasizing medieval Icelandic texts. This means that many of the ancient traditions are completely reimagined, and practitioners do not shy away from reinterpreting what some purists refer to as "classic" texts. Also, stressing Icelandic traditions and culture as opposed to Germanic history more generally accounts for the main difference within this religion. In fact, Asatru is modern Icelandic for "Æsir faith," meaning belief or loyalty to the major tribe of the Norse gods and goddesses. While practitioners usually refer to themselves as heathens, they will also openly share that their approach is slightly different.

Origins

This religious movement began in 1972 and was founded by Sveinbjorn Beinteinsson and a group of fellow Icelanders who decided it was important to bring back public worship of Norse gods and goddesses. Despite the once humble origins of this movement, it now has nearly forty thousand followers in one hundred countries worldwide.

It is important to note that while Asatruras do have a clergy, often referred to as *godar*. They do not have a central authority or dogma to follow. Followers of the Baha'i faith are the closest monotheistic iteration Astruars have since they also refused to make their religion dogmatic in any way, even as they believe in the central tenets that drive the heathen world.

Asatru has evolved since its first iteration in the 1970s to encompass a wide range of beliefs and practices essential to a modern way of life, including humanism and reconstructionism. They also tend to view the gods as metaphorical constructs, while others appreciate approaching them as distinct, powerful entities.

Three deities are widely believed to be the central organizing force in Asatru, Odin, Thor, and Freya. However, there is a large number of figures who also animate the distinct approach taken by practitioners. Also, a distinct feature of Asatru is that it emphasizes the importance of acting well and receiving rewards in this life, as opposed to waiting for the afterlife to reap any benefits. "We are our deeds" is an important aspect of Asatru, which is incredibly important to all its practitioners. As such, the Nine Noble Virtues is a vital part of the religion and serves as the driving force for all followers.

Nine Noble Virtues

The concept of the Nine Noble Virtues actually has a long history, and one version was thought to be devised by earlier heathens. It has been reinterpreted several times throughout history, but the last set was codified by Sveinbjorn Beinteinsson, the founder of Asatru, in the early 1970s. Broadly speaking, the Nine Noble Virtues are:

1. Courage
2. Truth
3. Honor
4. Fidelity
5. Discipline
6. Hospitality
7. Self-reliance
8. Industriousness
9. Perseverance

Later, followers of Asatru modified these simple yet arguably very broad concepts to include "Odinist values," which are more explicitly phrased moral or ethical guidelines. These are meant to offer some clear guidance on distinct moral quandaries that are not easily answered by the one-word dictates listed above. These Odinist values are:

- Strength is better than weakness
- Courage is better than cowardice
- Joy is better than guilt
- Honor is better than dishonor
- Freedom is better than slavery
- Kinship is better than alienation
- Realism is better than dogmatism
- Vigor is better than lifelessness
- Ancestry is better than rootlessness

Instead of residing solely in the world of moral absolutes, practitioners are given a very practical understanding of what's better than less desirable outcomes. There are other variations of these virtues as well, but in general, the central moral codes and worldview do not waver, and the idea is basically the same.

Rites and Festivals

There is some overlap between the rites and festivals that heathens and Asatruars enjoy, although the variations and intentions are clearly different.

For one, the blot is also an important occasion for those who follow Asatru but with a difference. While the blot here is also a rite intended to set out offerings to the gods, goddesses, and land spirits, they are also used to commemorate the dearly departed. It must be performed outside for dedicated followers, and an alcoholic substance is required. As always, mead is preferred, but beer and ale are also fine. In addition, the blot can be included in a festival held for a major holiday, such as midsummer or yule, and does not have to be performed independently.

The symbol is also important for followers, and the drinking ceremony is central. In this context, the symbol is perhaps less crucial than the blot, but it serves a vital function for followers since it is used as a way to establish one's identity and intent in a deeply sacred and traditional way. Despite the more flexible approach practitioners can take towards the symbol, there are a few well-established versions dedicated followers of Asatru take. In one version, people can drink three rounds. The first is dedicated to the gods, the second to great heroes of yore, the heroic figures from poems and sagas, and the third round would be an homage to the ancestors and friends who have passed from this world and have gone to the next.

Another popular way to perform the symbol is to pay respects to the past, present, and future. This ritual is meant to appreciate the parts of your past you'd like to mark, the things in your present you are thankful for, and elements of your future that you look forward to. Milestones, big and small, can be commemorated here in your own special way while also stating your hopes for the future. You can perform this sort of symbol with a small gathering of your closest friends or next of kin since it's meant to note something personal. While this version is less celebratory and more of a magical ritual, it is nonetheless important for followers of Asatru to perform from time to time.

Arguably the most important ceremony performed in Asatru is the profession. This is essentially a rite wherein you profess your belief in kinship and in the gods. It is usually performed to help mark an important moment in someone's life and state their understanding of their ancestors' power and earthly surroundings. This tends to be a very simple and short performance, but its poignancy is not lost on those who follow the religion. Even if it takes place in a regular meeting among practitioners, the simple act of loudly professing your beliefs among others is important. Sometimes the profession can be combined with the blot to help mark an especially important occasion.

Heathen or Asatruar?

Even though there could be some overlap, the differences between heathenry and Asatru are sometimes as clear as night and day. It's not really an either/or question, nor is one "better" or more authentic than the other. Both offer different roads for people to follow, especially those who are invested in preserving ancient ways of life. Interestingly, people adopt Asatru or heathenism for different reasons, and one reason could even be their political affiliation. Asatru has had an unfortunate moment in the sun lately due to neo-Nazis appropriating its central images and symbolism since anything with roots in Germanic culture is taken as a test for racial purity.

On the other end of the spectrum, you have a movement often referred to as "rainbow heathenry," which is a version that stresses openness to people of other ethnicities and gender identities and who engage in various forms of sexual expression without judgment. In this version, followers embrace a pre-Christian version of the world in which morality had less to do with sexual identity and more with ethical principles, similar to the Nine Noble Virtues described above.

Given that Norse spirituality is steeped in myth and symbols, it lends itself to interpretation by all sorts of people, which can sometimes lead to not-so-great results. That being said, there are hundreds of thousands of followers of both heathenry and Asatru throughout the world, and they are, by and large, devoted to the kinder aspects of the old ways. They are devoted to respecting elders and honoring the past while being deeply aware of the present. Many of us find ourselves unmoored by modernity, and technology has only hastened humankind's deepening sense of alienation. It's easy to get lost in the urban sprawl and the constant technological advances that are currently happening at breakneck speed, so it makes sense that people who find either Asatru or heathenry feel a tremendous sense of relief. They provide opportunities to slow down, listen to important tales and histories of the past, and create a strong, foundational moral core for people to follow.

Perhaps the main thing to note is that heathenism and Asatru should not be confused with Wicca, for example. Both, and perhaps especially heathenism, are influenced by literature and basic rituals, but magic rarely features in the equation. Furthermore, they differ greatly from most pagans in general in that they believe in each of the gods and goddesses as distinct entities and not as aspects of the overarching goddess whom Wiccans worship. They take polytheism seriously, as do ancient folktales and culture, and look for ways to bring them to life in the modern era. In all cases, these disparate groups have distinct theological backgrounds and differences, but they find commonalities in their shared desire to revive ancient practices that have long been suppressed with the advent of Christianity.

Chapter 5: Seiðr Magic and Shamanism

This chapter will dive deeper into one of the oldest magical practices of the Norse traditions – the art of Seiðr or Norse Shamanism. However, before delving into its background and, later on, the practical side of Seiðr magic, remember that shamanic practices take many years to master. For beginners, it's always a good idea to practice with an experienced guide who can teach you the basics of safe practices. Not only that, but they can help you learn to focus your mind on your intent. However, if you're unable to do this, whether due to temporary stress or an impoverished mental state, you shouldn't practice shamanism, as apart from focus, the process of Seiðr takes a lot of mental and spiritual energy. If your mental well-being isn't the best, to begin with, you won't have enough energy to successfully complete your work.

Smudging may be used to elevate the tension in your body and mind.
https://www.pexels.com/photo/a-bundle-of-sage-smoking-7947722/

What Is Shamanism?

Shamanism as a tradition has been present in human civilizations long before the Norse and Celtic cultures took over Europe and the rest of the world. Because of this, it's really tough to define what shamanism is. Evidence of shamanic practices has been found in cave paintings from the early Stone Age when the cultural development of human civilizations was still in its earlier stage. An overwhelming amount of evidence of similar practices came from the Iron Age when shamanism was already present in many different corners of the world. While somewhat similar in symbolism and techniques, the shamanic practices in each culture have already meant something different at this time. As human civilizations have evolved up until the modern days, so has the diversification of shamanic practices.

Shamanism is a set of practices through which one enters into an altered state of mind to journey to the spiritual world or contact one of its inhabitants. Typically, the journey or the contact is made with a specific intention, such as seeking advice, guidance, answers, and help with spiritual healing or growth. Other acts of shamans have included magical fears, visionary quests, weather working, shapeshifting, and divination.

How Is Shamanism Expressed in Norse Traditions?

Norse Shamanism has been practiced by the ancient Germanic tribes that had settled in Europe and, later on, the Norse people inhabiting Scandinavia. While very similar to Western Shamanism, the practice has been expressed slightly differently in Norse traditions. For starters, the foundation of Norse pagan practices has been built around the gods of the Norse pantheon, more specifically around Odin. According to Norse lore, Odin was one of the most powerful shamans. His work is evidenced in how he came upon the runes while hanging on Yggdrasill for nine days and nights without food, drinks, or sleep. It's still believed that Odin can help anyone enter an elevated state of mind and reveal the meaning of the runes. Odin's name is yet another proof of his ability to enter a trance needed for shamanic practices. The Old Norse word Óðinn is composed of the words "óðr," which means "inspiration" or "ecstasy," and the masculine suffix "-inn," which translates to the phrase "master of." When put together, these words mean "the master of ecstasy." Other myths suggest that Odin could also travel to the spiritual world before great battles to gather crucial knowledge he could use to secure victory. Other times he was said to make this journey for other people and deities while appearing asleep or being in a trance-like state. In a famous tale, Odin rode Sleipner (his eight-legged horse) to the otherworld to seek a seeress who could help his son. He would also travel to the underworld to consult with the spirits of the departed people and deities who have gathered great wisdom through their lives in the different worlds. It is believed that Odin relied on spiritual allies (often portrayed as two ravens) and taught the deities and people about the importance of learning from these guides. They showed him how to journey between worlds and gave him advice when needed, just as experienced shamans still do for beginners. Odin's trial during the discovery of the runes is also the basis for the shamanic tradition in which practitioners experience a symbolic death and revival before obtaining their abilities. However, one does not have to die physically and return to a new body. They could continue living in our world and travel between worlds even if they gained their power from a trance-like state.

That said, gaining runic insight was only Odin's first step in mastering shamanic practices. He learned the rest of the Seiðr from Freya, a goddess who originally belonged to another ancient tribe. This coincidentally highlights another notable difference between seidr and other forms of shamanism. In the early days, it was usually women who held this power. These women were called völva, seiðkona or seeresses. They would travel from village to village offering help, performing magic, divination, healing, and whatever was needed. Their spiritual guides led them to the place where their assistance was required. In return, they usually only asked for meals, housing, and similar forms of compensation. The few men who practiced shamanism worked in cults and were only concerned with wars, battles, and similar purposes, or worse, only with what they could personally gain. Whereas the völva looked out for the well-being of their entire community. Apart from healing and processes, it was their job to know how to find the best place for the tribe to hunt, spend the harsh winters, or plant the crops the tribe would harvest later in the year. According to Norse lore, the völva also could discern and shape the fated course of life of people by affecting it with magic. They would hang a few strings, pieces of shredded clothes, or plants and weave the fragments together, symbolically entering new, more desirable events into one's fate. Another way the seeresses prophesized was by spinning their staffs in their hands and entering an altered state of consciousness. Then, they would journey to Asgard or any other of the nine realms of the Norse world. According to certain myths, apart from bestowing blessings and helpful prophecies, the völva was also capable of enacting curses.

Another reason women were the only practitioners of Seiðr is that their abilities set them apart from the rest of society. While in most cases, they were highly respected (especially in the first couple of centuries CE), seeresses were also sometimes feared. When followers of other religions have begun to look into the shamanic practices, the völva often become reviled. They were forced to occupy less dignified roles than the rest of their tribe. Shamanic practices were often considered dishonorable, as were the people who practiced these. Men who worked with Seiðr were labeled as ergi (argr in Old Norse), which was a terrible insult amongst the Germanic tribes. Apart from the liberal way the women acted when traveling to wherever they felt called on, Seiðr was also considered ergi due to the weaving practice. Only women would want to meddle in fate and people's lives. It was considered unmanly to practice shamanism, which is why men were often shamed for it. Despite this, they are records of several men choosing Seiðr as a profession, presumably inspired by Odin and following his example. After all, the almighty Odin was labeled ergi too, but this didn't stop him from gathering a lot of power and spiritual wisdom. Some say that because of his shamanic practices, Odin could obtain the highest power in the universe. This knowledge was inspiring enough to disregard the ill-wishers who were only concerned with the current social norms and statuses.

Whether the practitioner of Seiðr was male or female, they were able to raise storms or invoke nightmares to stop their enemies and prevent them from entering into battle. They could also enact love spells and appear in the form of various animals to warn or guide people. When angered, the practitioners of Seiðr could provide false information about the future, make the land barren, and cause disasters. Journeying in an altered state of mind was standard practice and is one that has remained popular in modern times. One of the most popular acts of Seiðr is for the practitioner to sit on an elevated platform or within a sacred circle and enter into a trance-like state. During this, they seek out prophecies regarding themselves or others who require their help. Nowadays, more and more practitioners prefer journeying alone, although they do this after learning the act from an experienced teacher or spiritual guide. The journey often requires time for recovery afterward, as it can be exhausting for the body, mind, and spirit. The ancient shamans would also travel in the physical world, and not just when they were called. They would set out on a journey to find a source of spiritual wisdom, a better place for grounding, new tools, or whatever they felt they previously lacked. Sometimes, they needed to seek out a hidden item or information for healing, luck, or calling on the desired weather, animals to hunt, and so on. Other times they needed a new place for divination or a new ritual. They would usually take their trusted staff and roam the country until they were stopped, asked for assistance, or found what they were looking for. This is why they prefer to live in open places, apart from the rest of the people.

Another difference between the Norse and Western practices is how shamans enter an elevated state of mind. Western shamans typically require an elaborate ritual, complete with chanting or humming, drumming, and dancing, to elevate their minds from the mundane spiritual levels. In these cultures, shamanism is practiced in larger groups, even if it's only the shaman who does the journeying and collecting the information. In Seiðr, however, drumming, loud chanting, and dancing aren't necessary, although many practitioners enjoy singing and even a spinning motion. The act can be performed alone or in smaller groups, and the shaman relies most prevalently on their own ability to focus their intent on the task ahead. Some other tools they often use are a staff, a stool, or any elevated place for sitting, the spirits, and the spoken word (including prayers, songs, and chanting).

Techniques Based on the Seiðr Tradition

Modern techniques based on the Seiðr traditions vary depending on the practitioner's cultural and spiritual background and preferences for practicing magic. That said, below, you'll find the basic practices you can try to get started.

Cleansing and Other Preparations

Before you start any magical work, you'll need to cleanse your space, tools, and yourself. If you're working inside, a good way to purify everything is by smudging, i.e., smoking herbs with healing or other magical benefits. Besides banishing the negative energy from your working area, smudging may also be used to elevate the tension in your body and mind. If you're working outside, you'll only need to cleanse yourself, your tools, and the small area you'll be occupying (usually within a circle).

Prepare your tools - your staff, a chair for sitting, a blanket, and anything else you want to use. While a shaman's most powerful tool is their mind, you can use anything else that helps you focus on your work. After designating the area of magical work, you'll honor the cardinal directions, deities, spiritual guides, and nature spirits.

Grounding

Whether you're a beginner or an experienced practitioner performing an act of shamanic magic alone or within a group, the most crucial step to conquer is grounding. This means finding a connection to the energy of the universe and gaining the ability to harness its power. Seiðr requires intense focus, so you'll need all the help you can get. Grounding exercises will help you focus on your intent and form it in the first place. Whether you want to enact a spell, perform a ritual, journey to seek out information about the future, or do any other shamanic, you must root yourself in the present. Finding your place in the present will allow you to channel your thoughts in the right direction.

There are several ways to become grounded and focused on your magical tasks, and here are some you can try:

- **Using a staff:** Most practitioners use a staff to find a connection with nature and the universe. You'll need to find a quiet place outside and stand relaxed, holding the staff in your hand. Make sure it's upright and that it touches the ground. Take a few deep breaths, close your eyes, and allow your staff to channel energy until you find the connection.
- **Stomping:** Sometimes, simply touching the ground with your bare feet will be enough to make the connection. Other

times, you'll need to put more effort into this. For example, you can stomp on the ground until you feel focused. The stomping motion activates your power and nature's energy and chases away any thoughts unrelated to what you're doing in the present moment.

- **Sitting on rocks and other natural landmarks**: These can make a powerful connection to nature and the universe itself, so if you have a chance to find them in your vicinity, go ahead and sit on them. If not, you can sit on the ground too. Either way, your feet should keep touching the ground. This will allow you to find and maintain a connection with the present.

Casting Circle

Whether an act is performed alone or in a group, most practitioners agree that a sacred circle is one of the most powerful magical tools you can use. Casting circles allows you to create sacred space anywhere you choose. Just like grounding, forming the circle focuses your mind on your intent. Within this circle, you can harness more power and protect yourself from malicious intentions and spirits. This is particularly important when you're in a trance and lose complete focus of your surroundings or the ability to actively defend yourself from bad vibes. To make a casting circle, you will need to:

- Trace the boundaries of the area you want the circle to occupy. You can do this by placing objects around the perimeter. Rocks and crystals work the best, but you can also use any other tools to which you feel drawn.
- Cleanse the space inside the circle. To ensure that only positive energy remains around you, you can cleanse the circle by smudging or banishing negative energy with your words.
- Walk around the perimeter and visualize the borders becoming shrouded in bright light to feel even more secure. You can also hold out your staff in front of you and point it towards the boundaries as you walk clockwise. As the light around you burns, it will also help cleanse the circle.
- You can call on any deity or spiritual guide you want to work with and visualize them entering the circle too.

- Take a few deep breaths, and focus on the magical energy coursing through your body. Feel how it expands with every breath you release, as it falls under the influence of your connection with your guides and the universe.
- When you feel your power connecting with energy emanating from the circle's edges, say, "*My work now begins, and the circle is now cast.*"
- Perform your work and close your circle by walking in the opposite direction.

Entering a Trance

To enter into a trance, you'll need your mind to be detached from your daily preoccupations and open to whatever messages you may receive. This will allow you to interpret the information correctly and use the wisdom you've received daily. Novice practitioners are advised to practice solitary Seiðr alongside an experienced guide. This means addressing only your own questions and not queries from a group of people.

The best place to try reaching an elevated state of mind is outdoors in nature. For the best effects, go outside just before sunset. Being in the dark will help keep distractions to a minimum. Take your staff with you. Start forming your intention when you leave your home by channeling it into your staff. The intent should be as clear-cut as possible and intensive enough to generate a powerful message. Think about your intention like you would about a pressing question you're entertaining during a conversation with a friend. While the spiritual language is universal, you'll need to ensure they understand you correctly and that you'll be able to understand their response too.

When you reach and prepare your space, take a few deep breaths and start focusing on the intention you've formed. There are several ways to do this, including meditation, rocking back and forth, breathing deeply, reciting poetry, or, most popularly, singing. Choose a method you feel drawn to. You'll know you've reached the elevated state when instead of the stimuli from our world, you suddenly start receiving any that don't belong in your current setting. These may be images, sounds, or anything else your senses may pick up. Don't question the messages you receive until you finish your work.

Chapter 6: Working with the Goddess Freyja

Now that you understand a little more about Seiðr Magic and Norse Shamanism, it's essential to look at it in further detail, especially if you're interested in working with the goddess Freyja.

The goddess Freyja.
Eden, Janine and Jim from New York City, CC BY 2.0
<https://creativecommons.org/licenses/by/2.0>, via Wikimedia Commons:
https://commons.wikimedia.org/wiki/File:Freyja_(4956074-0206).jpg

In this chapter, we'll explore the idea of shamanic journeys in further detail and help you understand some shamanic journeys undertaken by figures from Norse spirituality. However, before you can go further in your shamanic journey and understand how to contact the goddess Freyja, you must first understand who she is.

The Goddess Freyja

In Norse mythology, the goddess Freyja was a member of the Vanir rather than the Aesir. The Vanir were another "tribe" of gods and goddesses in Norse spirituality, with the most prominent (and best-known) "tribe" being the Aesir of Asgard.

However, Freyja was not only a member of the Vanir but also an honorary member of the Aesir. She was the goddess of love, fertility, and beauty. Her family included Njord, her father, and Freyr, her brother.

In some stories, Freyja is married to the obscure god Odr. However, many scholars link Odr to Odin and Freyja herself to Frigg, Odin's wife.

As the goddess of beauty, Freyja was considered the "most glorious" of all the Norse goddesses. She was the mistress and ruler of Fólkvangr, one of the afterlives in Norse mythology.

As the mistress of Fólkvangr, Freyja received half of the souls of all Norse people who died in battle. The other half traveled to Valhalla. However, the major difference between Fólkvangr and Valhalla is that Fólkvangr is also open to women who died a "noble death," while Valhalla was only open to warriors who died in battle.

Because Freyja is the mistress of Fólkvangr, some scholars consider her to be a war goddess as well as the goddess of beauty. In fact, they consider her to be a Valkyrie and perhaps the most prominent Valkyrie of them all.

Some attributes of Freyja noted in existing mythology include:

- She owned the mythical torc/necklace, *Brísingamen*, made of gold. In one story, it was stolen by Loki, who had transformed into a seal to do so.
- Cats were sacred to her, and her chariot was drawn by these animals. Other sacred animals to Freyja included pigs and

boars. In fact, she also rode a boar with golden bristles.

- Her mother is unknown. Depending on the source, she may have been a sister of Njord, the giantess/goddess of winter Skadi, or Nerthus, the Norse/Germanic version of Mother Earth.

The most prominent myth that involves Freyja involves the theft of the god Thor's hammer, Mjölnir, by the giant Thrym. After Loki discovers the source of the theft, Thrym agrees to return the hammer to Thor as long as he is permitted to marry Freyja.

In one version of the story, Thor tells Freyja to dress as a bride and go with him to meet Thrym. However, on hearing this, Freyja is incensed and refuses to do so, saying that she would be the "lewdest of women" if she agreed.

So, the gods meet to discuss getting Thor's hammer back. At the end of the discussion, Thor agrees to dress up as and pretend to be Freyja in an effort to fool the giant and win his hammer back – a trick that is, ultimately, successful.

Freyja as the First Völva

Aside from her role in Norse myths, Freyja is also known as the first völva.

Along with her brother and father, Freyja became an honorary member of the Aesir following the end of the Aesir and Vanir wars. Their honorary Aesir status also ensured that there would be no future wars that would break out between the two "tribes" of deities.

Following her transition from Vanaheim to Asgard, Freyja taught the Aesir the art of Seiðr Magic. She was the first of the Norse shamans, even before Odin, and in her role as the völva of Asgard and Vahaeim, she was venerated by mortal völvas.

There is evidence that a völva buried around 1000 BC was buried with a silver pendant with a figure that likely represented Freyja wearing her torc Brísingamen.

As a practitioner of Seiðr Magic, Freyja understood the workings of fate and how to use that understanding to change fate. In some accounts, Freyja is considered to be greedy and evil for teaching the other gods how to perform Seiðr Magic.

However, Seiðr Magic is a twofold ability. While it can be used to create negative consequences for the victim of a practitioner, it can also be used to bring about positive change. While, in some stories, the ability to wield Seiðr Magic is considered to be evil, it is more commonly a neutral ability whose direction is dictated by the user.

There are hints throughout Norse myths of the power that Freyja was able to wield as the first practitioner of Seiðr Magic. For example, in one story, Freyja is able to transform into a falcon with the help of falcon feathers that she owns. She can also lend these feathers (in some stories, these are not individual feathers, rather, they are part of a cloak of feathers) to allow them to change their shape. For example, she lends these feathers/cloak to Loki to help him discover the culprit behind the theft of Thor's hammer, Mjölnir.

Additionally, there is also the role of Freyja as the wife of Odr.

In one of the few stories that survive about the god Odr, he travels away from the other gods. Where and why he goes has not survived – only the fact that he leaves. Freyja, who loves her husband, searches for him but cannot find him. In her anguish, she cries tears of gold as she continues her search.

For some scholars, Freyja's search for Odr represents an early version of the shamanic journey. Additionally, as Odr is associated with Odin (and Freyja with Frigg), there is a possibility that this tale represents a story where Freyja/Frigg go in search of Odr/Odin during the period when Odin goes on his own shamanic journey, hanging himself from a branch of Yggdrasil as part of his discovery of runes.

Additionally, stories say that Odin traveled extensively to distant lands. This may, once again, be why Freyja/Frigg was called to travel in search of Odr/Odin, going on her own shamanic journey parallel to her husband's.

Freyja's Powers in Relation to Other Deities

It's essential to note that while Freyja was the first völva, she was not the most powerful.

That honor rested with the Norns.

The Norns were generally represented by a group of three women who wove the fate of mortals and gods. Even Odin was forced to consult with the Norns when he wanted to discern his own future.

As the weavers of fate, the Norns were the most powerful völvas and the most powerful wielders of Seiðr Magic.

Understanding the Shamanic Journey

It is essential to note that in Norse Shamanism, the journey taken by the völva was different from the shamanic journey.

Völvas were generally women. Norse shamans, on the other hand, were both men and women, and this distinction meant that rituals between völvas and shamans differed.

The major known ritual of a völva is that of the prophecy.

Völvas were traveling women who traveled from community to community, likely with a group of young women. She would visit a community when called to help with prophesying important information, such as when a famine would end or when the rain would arrive.

After arriving at a community, the völva would take the time to understand the community and its environment. After that, she would be fed a feast of animal hearts. The hearts would come from as many different types of animals as could be found in the environment.

It is possible that the animals killed for the völva's feast were part of a ritual sacrifice, the information about which has not survived. Additionally, others likely ate the meat from the animals killed for the feast, possibly the women she traveled with or community members.

After eating her feast, it was time for the völva to make a prophecy.

As part of the prophecy ritual, the völva was seated on a special cushion that was made with hen feathers. Following this, a special song was sung to enable her to enter a prophesied trance. The song helped summon spirits, which the völva would use to make her prophecy.

She would use the information imparted to her by the spirits to answer the question(s) posed to her by the community. Most commonly, the völva was summoned to help prophecy the end of famines. If left unchecked, they could devastate communities and kill scores of people.

That said, this was a ritual used only by the völvas. For the Norse shamans, the shamanic journey involved other steps that resembled the ones Odin took during his shamanic journey to find and reveal the knowledge of runes.

As part of the shamanic journey, purification was carried out using sacred herbs. The herbs were used to eliminate distractions that might draw the shaman's attention away from the journey they were undertaking.

The space to be purified would be determined by the leader of the group of shamans – generally, the person who would be undertaking the journey. The process of going on a shamanic journey as part of Norse Shamanism and the practice of Seiðr Magic was not a solo one. Rather, it was performed by a group of participants.

Once the space where the journey was to take place was purified, the next step was to call on the directions, the nature spirits, and the gods. When calling on the gods, special attention was paid to the deities associated with Seiðr Magic, such as Odin, Freyja, and the Norns.

It should be noted that this procedure was not necessary for taking a shamanic journey, and it is possible to go through a journey without undergoing this level of ritual. However, these ritual steps ensure that everyone involved in the journey is fully involved in the process and is not distracted by other concerns. In essence, it served a psychological purpose rather than a practical one.

Once the area was prepared, the journey started with ritual words. After the ritual words were spoken, the participants began drumming, chanting, and singing. The energy created by doing this was transferred to the shaman, who could then use it as part of their journey.

One member of the participants (generally the drummer) acted as a guide, helping the shaman on their journey. The drum beat helped determine how the shaman proceeded on their journey, and the guide also provided instructions on what the shaman should do.

As the journey started, the shaman would relax their body, breathe deeply, and start visualizing their journey. The mental journey would take place in the Sacred Grove, which formed the gateway between the mortal and spirit worlds. The Sacred Grove is the home of Yggdrasil, the World Tree.

From the Sacred Grove, the shaman travels down Yggdrasil to the Underworld/Hel. They do not enter the Underworld immediately, not being dead themselves; rather, they stand before the Gate of the Underworld, asking their questions and letting the spirits answer them.

While the shaman undertakes their spiritual journey, the guide continues to narrate it to the other participants. This way, all the people participating are able to vicariously experience the shaman's journey.

Once the other participants have completed their own symbolic journeys and arrive at the Gate to the Underworld with the shaman, he can enter the Underworld. This is the second part of the ritual, the part that only the shaman will undertake.

Once the shaman enters the Underworld, their experience is unique to each person. Some shamans will ask questions out loud, others will visualize them, and so on.

After the shaman has the answers they were looking for, the guide will signal the start of the end of the journey. At this point, the observers will ask their questions verbally to the shaman. Questions must be as simple and specific as possible to allow the shaman to provide a specific answer.

The guide also keeps an eye on the shaman, helping to end the question session if they notice fatigue. As part of the questioning session, the shaman may also channel the spirits of the dead, although this depends entirely on the spirits and the questions asked of them.

Once the questions have been answered or the shaman tires, the guide helps him make the journey back to the mortal world. If more questions are answered, the process may be repeated for a second shaman, then a third, and so on. This depends on the number of questions to be asked and the number of shamans present.

As the last one makes the journey back home, the guide narrates the return journey as they make the journey to the Underworld. This allows the observers to return from their own journeys and signals an end to the ritual of the shamanic journey. Once the journey is over, the observers, shaman, and guide must all eat and drink to replenish their energy.

Journeying to Freyja

As modern Seiðr Magic practitioners, your first shamanic journey should be to meet Freyja. Not only is she the First Völva as the teacher of Seiðr Magic, but she is also the First Shaman.

As part of your shamanic journey to meet Freyja, you must first meditate on her to connect with her before you can attempt a proper shamanic journey.

To meditate on Freyja, you should:

- Choose an essential oil blend that you like or that aligns with Freyja. Some options you can consider include lemon verbena, geranium, lime, and jasmine.
- Apply some of the oil to the palm of your hand. The left hand is the better option, though you can use your right hand as well, depending on what you're most comfortable with.
- Inhale the scent of the essential oil to begin your meditation.
- Close your eyes and let your worries fall away. Once you're relaxed, call on your guide and guardians, as well as the spirits of the four directions and elements, to help guide you during your meditation.
- Put forth your intention with this meditation – to connect with the goddess Freyja, the first shaman. Put forth these intentions to Nerthus, a potential mother of Freyja and the representation of Mother Earth.
- Call upon the goddess Freyja, thanking her for her presence. Give yourself the space to connect with her consciousness, allowing yourself to bask in her presence and appreciate her dual roles at the First Völva and First Shaman.
- Once you're done with your meditation, thank the spirits who have helped you connect with Freyja and let go of the energy you're holding on to.

Once you've connected with Freyja, you can then start practicing for your shamanic journey. Remember, you will need someone to act as a guide, so you must choose your companion carefully.

Now that you understand how to connect with Freyja and practice to undertake a shamanic journey, the next step is to understand how to travel through Yggdrasil during this journey.

Chapter 7: Journeying through Yggdrasill

A sacred giant living ash tree that holds the universe together and lies at its heart. Deities and humans have been drawn to the World Tree, Yggdrasill, since time immemorial. Because everything leads back to Yggdrasil, the tree holds great spiritual value to many. It is easily the most important entity in Norse traditions.

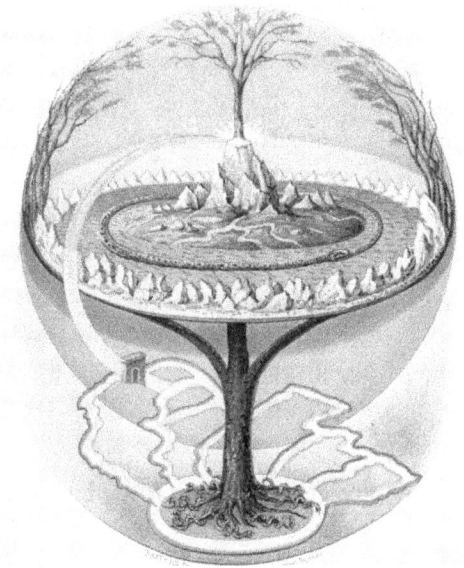

Because everything leads back to Yggdrasil, the tree holds great spiritual value to many.
https://commons.wikimedia.org/wiki/File:Yggdrasil.jpg

Being the root of the entire universe, the majestic tree holds the answers to many questions. That's what the deities and wise men that once roamed the Earth thought. Following their footsteps, you can also attempt to unravel the tree's power and mystery and walk among the gods.

Before you do that, take this opportunity to contemplate the magnificence of Yggdrasill and its significance to the cosmos. This chapter will explore that and guide you through a wonderful journey through the realms surrounding Yggdrasil.

The Story behind Yggdrasill

The closest thing to Yggdrasill in other religions and mythologies is the Tree of Life concept. Trees are sacred in countless beliefs and are seen as symbols of life, rebirth, knowledge, and the cyclical nature of the universe, among other things.

While Yggdrasill represents similar concepts, it also supports the entire universe and is a sacred place to both deities and humans. The gods would assemble at its base every day and watch over the realms. Many kinds of creatures lurk in several parts of the tree.

How Yggdrasill came into existence is not known. It may have always existed, but several things suggest that it is mortal, which we'll cover later on. Naturally, Yggdrasill's well-being is linked to that of the universe. What we do know, however, is that it is a powerful symbol and an accurate depiction of the cycle of nature. It may be in a different plane of existence altogether, but it possesses incredible energy that draws in both gods and humans.

The Center of the Cosmos

The universe comprises nine realms, all spread out from Yggdrasil's branches and roots and occupying different levels. The tree's branches stretch far above the heavens. Yggdrasill is referred to as "the friend of the clear sky" in the old Völuspá poem. The roots reach into the underworld realms.

Because Yggdrasil is the center of the universe, journeying through the realms takes place through it. The way the world is arranged around Yggdrasil is not always clear, but the tree definitely connects all parts of the world. We'll cover the realms surrounding Yggdrasil in more detail later on.

The Tree of Wisdom: Odin's Sacrifices

Besides being the very center of the universe, Yggdrasil is associated with wisdom and knowledge. Odin was absolutely relentless in his pursuit of knowledge. For a long time, he observed the well of Urd from which Yggdrasill grows. He saw that Mimir, who had unparalleled wisdom, often drank from the well. Seeking enlightenment and wisdom, Odin set out to drink from the well but had to sacrifice an eye in return, which he did.

The well is home to powerful creatures known as the Norns, who created and controlled the fates of all beings, including gods. They did this by carving runes that were then carried throughout Yggdrasill. Determined to figure out the secret behind the runes, Odin pierced himself with a spear, hung himself from one of the tree's branches, and kept staring down at the well for nine days until the runes finally revealed themselves to him.

Because of Odin's divine sacrifice, Yggdrasill is seen as a source of cosmic knowledge, wisdom, and enlightenment.

Ragnarök: A New Beginning

The fate of Yggdrasill and the universe are intertwined. While Yggdrasill has always existed, it is not immortal, and its downfall may signal the universe's destruction. Its mortality is perhaps symbolized by the four stags continually feeding from it and bringing it closer to decay. Therefore, the tree needs compassion and protection to nourish life.

Yggdrasill plays a crucial role in the events of Ragnarök, but its fate remains unclear. Come Ragnarök, there will be chaos all around. The sky will split, the stars will disappear, the realms will be destroyed, and Yggdrasill will tremble. Most gods, demons, giants, and humans will die in Ragnarök.

Yggdrasill will quaver and will seem to fall and end life as we know it, particularly when Surtr, the fire giant, flings his fire and almost ravages it to the ground. However, it will endure and signal a new beginning for humankind. Yggdrasill's trunk will provide shelter for the surviving gods as well as the two last humans, Líf and Lífþrasir.

From there, a new universe will emerge, and life will continue in a world free of chaos.

The World around Yggdrasill

Yggdrasill stands in the very middle of the Norse universe and is the bridge connecting all parts of the world.

The Nine Realms

Yggdrasill is the cosmic tree that extends to the farthest reaches of the universe and holds the nine realms within its roots and branches.

1. **Asgard:** Home to the Æsir gods and goddesses, Asgard is where the gates to the great halls of Valhalla are located. This realm is believed to be high up in the sky and connected to the realm of humankind via a rainbow bridge.

2. **Vanaheim:** Just as the Æsir settled in Asgard, the Vanir deities established their home in Vanaheim. While there is no clear description of what the Vanaheim is like, it is probably a magical and fertile realm since the Vanir are associated with sorcery, magic, and nature.

3. **Alfheim::** Ruled by the Vanir God Freyr, Alfheim is the homeland of the Ljósálfar, light elves who were described as "fairer than the sun to look at" in the Prose Edda. The light elves are considered patrons of art, poetry, and music. Alfheim is thought to be located in the heavens along with Asgard and Vanaheim.

4. **Jotunheim:** The sworn enemies of the Æsir gods are the Jötnar, or giants, who inhabit the chaotic realm of Jotunheim. The realm is thought to be separated from Asgard by the eternally flowing river of Ífingr that is almost impossible to cross. One of Yggdrasil's great roots extends to Mimir's well, located in Jotunheim.

5. **Midgard:** The home of humankind, this lies in the middle of the world and around Yggdrasill. Surrounding Midgard is a vast impassable ocean guarded by the World Serpent Jörmungandr, child of Loki and the giantess Angrboða. Midgard was fashioned by Odin and his brothers Vili and Vé from the body parts of the giant Augelmir, the ancestor of all Jötnar and the

very first being in the universe.

6. **Svartalfheim/Nidavellir**: This cold, dark realm is the home of the dwarves, known for their immense magic and craftsmanship abilities. This is where Mjölnir, Thor's infamous hammer, was forged. Odin's magical golden ring, Draupnir, and his spear, Gungnir, were also crafted by the dwarves in Nidavellir.

7. **Muspelheim**: Back when nothing else but Yggdrasil and the void of Ginnungagap existed, the fire realm Muspelheim and the dark, icy, misty realm Niflheim were the first to come into existence. Muspelheim is home to the fire giants, led by Surtr, the arch nemesis of the Æsir.

8. **Niflheim**: On the opposite side of the universe from Muspelheim lies the primordial land of fog and mist known as Niflheim. The dark, cold realm is home to the eleven freezing-cold rivers of Élivágar, stemming from the wellspring Hvergelmir. One of Yggdrasill's roots extends all the way to Hvergelmir. Niflheim, along with Muspelheim, is seen as the origin of all living beings. The giant Ymir, who is the first being in the universe, was created when the ice of Niflheim mixed with the fire of Muspelheim.

9. **Hel:** Ruled over by the goddess or giantess Hel, another child of Loki and Angrboða, Hel is the Norse underworld where all those unworthy of Valhalla are cast. Hel's location sometimes overlaps with that of Niflheim. Hel is also said to be beneath the root of Yggdrasill that extends to Hvergelmir. However, the two realms are described very differently in Norse mythology.

The link between Yggdrasill and the nine realms is undeniable and acts as a powerful symbol, that is, the interconnectivity of all the universe's elements. With that in mind, how the various worlds are arranged around Yggdrasill is difficult to decide. For instance, little is known about some of the realms and how they can be reached. Journeying through the realms was reserved only for the most intrepid of travelers, gods or otherwise. Several paths separating realms are well-known. Even those are impossible to cross, except for a very few beings.

Several attempts have been made to reconstruct Norse cosmology. The realms are thought by many to spread out from the branches of Yggdrasill. Consequently, they will lie on different levels. Based on this view of the Norse universe, the realms of Asgard, Vanaheim, and Alfheim occupy the highest level and constitute the heavens. Midgard is in the middle, and along with it are Jotunheim and Nidavellir. The lowest level represents the underworld and includes Muspelheim, Niflheim, and Helheim. Yggdrasill has three great roots extending to Jotunheim, up towards Asgard, and down to Niflheim.

Another approach acknowledges these 3 levels but suggests that the realms are all beneath Yggdrasill. Similarly, Yggdrasill's roots extend to each level, reaching Asgard, Jotunheim, and Niflheim.

The Creatures of Yggdrasill

A variety of fantastic beasts lurk in and around Yggdrasill. At the very top of the tree sits an unnamed eagle and a hawk known as Veðrfölnir. Underneath the lowermost root in Niflheim is a monstrous serpent named Níðhöggr, who continuously eats away at the root. A squirrel named Ratatoskr runs up and down Yggdrasill and carries messages between the eagle and the serpent. Four stags named Dvalinn, Dáinn, Duneyrr, and Duraþrór move around the tree branches and nibble on its leaves, while the Norns of the Well of Urdr in Asgard (the well holds one of Yggdrasill's roots) keep healing and nourishing the tree. In the ocean surrounding Midgard lurks the World Serpent Jörmungandr, often depicted as circling around Yggdrasill.

The Wells of Yggdrasill

Yggdrasill is watered by three sacred wells that play a significant role in Norse mythology. Each well is located in a path connecting Yggdrasill and a specific realm.

Urðarbrunnr, or the Well of Urðr

The fate of all creation is decided by the Norns that inhabit the well of Urdr. It is located beneath Yggdrasill's root in Asgard and where the gods are thought to assemble daily. The Well of Urdr is the setting of Odin's ultimate sacrifice that led him to unravel the secret behind the runes.

Mímisbrunn, or Mimir's Well

One of the three Yggdrasill's roots extends to Mimir's well, located in the realm of the giants, Jotunheim. As the name suggests, the well is guarded by Mimir, a figure with immense knowledge and wisdom achieved by drinking from the well. Mimir's well is the central element of Odin's eye sacrifice mentioned earlier in the chapter.

Hvergelmir

Yggdrasill's third great root extends all the way down to Niflheim, precisely at the Hvergelmir. The wellspring is the first source of water that came into existence and is a crucial element in the creation of the very first being, the giant Ymir. Hvergelmir is home to a large number of snakes as well as the serpent Níðhöggr, who keeps gnawing at the root of Yggdrasill.

Your First Journey through Yggdrasill

By now, you're familiar with the significance of Yggdrasill and can set the scene for a journey of self-discovery and enlightenment. Following the footsteps of Odin, the epitome of spiritual journeying, you can also aim to attain higher consciousness and spiritual awareness through Yggdrasill and its surrounding realms.

Yggdrasill houses all aspects of life and consciousness. It encompasses powerful energy and is shrouded in mystery that does not unravel easily, not even for the likes of Odin. Such a journey requires a great deal of curiosity, devotion, and patience.

Balancing Your Energies

Before your cosmic journey, you must be well-prepared physically and mentally. This can be achieved by various meditative practices, both old and new. The aim is to balance your inner energies and clear your mind of all distractions, making it easier to channel the right energy for your journey.

An efficient practice to attain a state of relaxation is through grounding, a traditional Norse Magic practice, which you can perform in honor of Jörð, the mother of Thor and the personification of Earth. The best way to ground yourself to Jörð would be outdoors in nature, ideally with your bare feet touching the ground.

Close your eyes and visualize your distractions being pushed down through your body to your feet and into the ground. Take slow deep breaths in the process, as this will help you cleanse your mind faster. Afterward, visualize drawing the Earth's vital energy to your body. Stay as relaxed and focused as you can, and let Jörð's energy flow through every part of your body. By the time you're done, you should feel refreshed and transformed, which will aid you in your journey.

Interpreting Yggdrasill and the Nine Realms

Depictions of Yggdrasill and the Norse universe are plenty. You can make your journey far more illustrious through the power of imagery. One of the best ways to enhance your journey is by setting up an indoor or outdoor altar. To represent Yggdrasill, you can use tree branches and leaves, preferably from evergreens like ash. A drawing or a model of Yggdrasill also works.

Around your representation of the tree, consider lighting candles, especially if you're inside your home. In Norse traditions, candles are powerful ritual elements and can help you work better with spirits to ease your journey. Upon learning about each realm and its figures and symbols, you can associate each realm with a specific color and choose your candle colors accordingly.

You can also place offerings of rocks, crystals, runes, and herbs with medicinal and magical properties around the altar. Your altar will help you visualize your journey and know what you're looking for. Keep in mind that your journey will be unique, and so should your altar.

Opening the Doors of Perception

Your voyage through Yggdrasill and its nine realms is a path toward an elevated state of consciousness. By creating a suitable setting, you can enter an ecstatic trance that can open your mind to wonderful revelations about yourself and the world around you. Several things can enhance your state of trance.

Drumming Journey

Drums are used in many Norse rituals and are known to have various uses, including healing, ceremonies, journeying between worlds, and invoking spirits. The rhythmic beat of Shamanic journey drums has a powerful effect and can help alter your perception and increase the likelihood of communing with helping spirits.

Runic Chanting

Chanting the runes is a powerful traditional Norse ritual and is a crucial element in Galdr magic, which we'll cover in more detail in a later chapter. It is a powerful spell incantation that helps you enter a state of trance. You can focus on a few runes at a time and chant their names, preferably along the shamanic drum beats. For this purpose, you should familiarize yourself with the meaning and symbolism of runes to help you choose the runes to be chanted.

Runes are important elements that allude to Odin's divine sacrifice in Yggdrasill. There are no wrong ways to choose your runes as long as they are of significance to you. While chanting the runes, it's important to visualize or reflect on their meaning. Runes are a great source of insight and can be a recurring image in your journey.

Making Your Path

By now, you're likely to notice changes in your perception and find yourself completely focused and immersed in your experience. Even then, you can still use the help of spiritual guides that you can call at any time. Spirits are often of great help to those who reach out to them. As long as your intentions are clear and well-formulated, you can allow yourself to be guided by spirits. The practice of Seiðr can be very useful at this stage.

Your journey through Yggdrasill should be one of ascension and transformation. Try to visualize yourself at the root that extends all the way down to Hvergelmir in Niflheim. Acknowledge and embrace the darkness of the underworld realms and the vile creatures that nibble away at Yggdrasill. After reflecting on that, you can make your way up to the middle realms where giants, dwarves, and humans dwell. These realms represent our everyday perception of reality and are crucial in understanding who we are and our place in the universe. From there, carve your path toward the heavenly realms that exist on the highest plane of consciousness in the universe.

Make sure to spend as much time as possible exploring, contemplating, and honoring the experience. Don't hesitate to ask your helping spirits for guidance and stay connected to them for as long as the journey takes. Whichever path you've been taken into, embrace it and come out as a transformed being. Put the insights you gain to good use in your everyday life.

Chapter 8: Norse Runes 101

This chapter discusses the origins of the runes and how they were used in ancient times. After reading it, you'll learn their English and phonetic equivalents and their meanings. While runes as an alphabet aren't used in modern languages, you'll receive plenty of advice on how to use them to write modern texts, starting with a few simple words and sentences. Just like runic meditation, this will help you familiarize yourself with the shape and energy of the runes. This knowledge will come in handy in runic divination and similar rune magic practices.

The Origins of the Runes

According to Norse lore, the runes were revealed to people by the deities. The first who came upon them was Odin after he hung from the Yggdrasil, the World Tree, for 9 days and nights without food, water, or sleep. After learning about their magical power, Odin decided to share the runes with everyone else, allowing their wisdom to be harnessed for different purposes. Runic inscriptions were found on the belongings of Germanic tribes that lived around 50 CE.

The earliest known record of the first complete set of runes dates to around 400. This was the first runic alphabet, known as "Futhark" by the Norse. The name of the alphabet is derived from its first letters. These were Fehu, Uruz, Thurisaz, Ansuz, Raidho, and Kenaz. This first runic alphabet was called Elder Futhark and was used until the 8th century. It consisted of 24 runes, divided into three aettir, the groups ruled over by prominent Norse deities. The first runes of each ættir (Fehu, Hagalaz, and Tiwaz) are also called the Mother Runes because they were believed to be the first additions to the Elder Futhark. In addition, the other runes in their respective groups can be tied to them phonetically. This is evidence of how the entire alphabet was used as a phonetic system rather than a written form of the spoken Norse language.

In Scandinavia, the Elder Futhark was shortened to 16 runes, becoming the Younger Futhark. Unlike its predecessor, this alphabet was easier to use. The runes were less complex, and there weren't any harsh lines involved in their carving. In other parts of Europe, the Elder Futhark changed into Anglo-Saxon Futhorc (used until the 11th century) and later the Medieval Futhark (used from the 12th to the 15th century).

How Runes Were Used in Ancient Times

Both written and oral records confirm that the ancient Germanic tribes used the runes for several purposes. For starters, the runes were their written form of communication. The most educated members of the tribes recorded each significant event by carving the runes and inscribing them into stone or wood. At first, runes were carved into massive stone monuments, testifying to the tribe's achievements. Later, they became smaller objects, which the people could take with them as they traveled. They also started to incorporate runes into art and clothes manufacturing and were then taken over by the followers of other religions.

Besides a writing tool, the runes were also used for magical practices. They were into folk magic work with Celtic origins, such as divination and spiritual communication. They are believed to be infused with natural magic. Each carries a slightly different spiritual substance. Due to their magical essence, runes could foster communication between all that's encompassed by the universal spirit. They could also take on a person or being's own magic, which allowed for more efficient communication.

As knowledge of the runes began to spread among the population, there was confusion about their use. Those who only had a rudimentary understanding of their magical side often used runes for the wrong purposes, causing more harm than good, even if this wasn't their intention.

The Meaning of the Elder Futhark Runes

The runes in the Elder Futhark alphabet have several meanings. Most of these are tied to natural forces. These can change and evolve with time, just as nature does through each cycle. Consequently, the interpretation of each rune depends on how it's affected by these changes at any given time. That said, several runic correspondences are just as relevant as they were in ancient times. Here is what each rune in the Elder Futhark alphabet means in modern English, alongside their phonetic equivalent and modern pronunciation.

Freyr's Aett

As the son of the sea God Njörd, Freyr is one of the most prominent deities of the Norse pantheon. He is the god of fertility, peace, and new beginnings. The runes in his aett represent creativity, finding your way to establish material security and the early stages of spiritual development.

ᚠ - Fehu

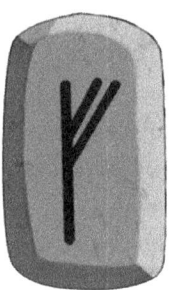

Fehu.
https://pixabay.com/es/illustrations/fehu-runa-fe-runa-adivinaci%c3%b3n-6508602/

Modern phoneme: F
English pronunciation: "FAY-hoo"

Fehu, in English, means cattle or wealth. However, it can also illustrate the realization of dreams and significant goals, good luck, material gain, and property, not to mention hope for improving one's life.

ᚢ - Uruz

Uruz.
https://pixabay.com/es/illustrations/uruz-ur-runa-futhark-n%c3%b3rdico-6508604/

Modern phoneme: U
English pronunciation: "OO-rooz"

Uruz is translated as "bull" or "wild ox." Representing the power of this animal, this rune is linked to perseverance, endurance, willpower, physical health, and vitality. It also reveals more goals to be achieved and challenges to be overcome through courageous behavior.

ᚦ - Thurisaz

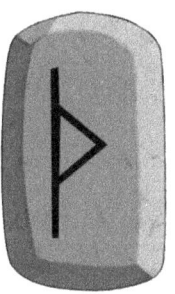

Thurisaz.
https://pixabay.com/es/illustrations/thurisaz-jueves-runa-futhark-6508603/

Modern phoneme: Th
English pronunciation: "THUR-ee-sazh"

This rune is translated as "giant" or "thorn" in English. It's also the universal Norse symbol for the hammer of Thor. Like the hammer, the rune illustrates protection and defense. At the same time, it can point to danger, disruptive forces, or conflict. Thurisaz means purification, and cathartic forces bring divine wisdom.

ᚠ - Ansuz

Ansuz.
https://pixabay.com/es/illustrations/ansuz-runa-runas-futhark-2644294/

Modern phoneme: A
English Pronunciation: "AHN-sooz"

The meaning of Ansuz is revelation or message. It is linked to several Norse deities, including Odin, the master of communication. The rune indicates messages and insight one may receive through visions and signs. It also represents everything that has to do with oral communication, including the mouth and the vocal cords.

ᚱ - Raidho

Raidho.
https://pixabay.com/es/illustrations/raidho-runa-runas-futhark-2644605/

Modern phoneme: R
English pronunciation: "Rah-EED-ho"

The literal meaning of this rune is "traveling on horseback" or simply "journey." In broad terms, Raidho can also represent any form of movement or progress in life, including finding new perspectives and spiritual growth. It may also refer to intuitively channeling your energy, working on goals, and making better decisions.

‹ - Kenaz

Kenaz.
https://pixabay.com/es/illustrations/kenaz-runa-runas-futhark-2644856/

Modern phoneme: C / K
English pronunciation: "KEN-ahz"

Kenaz has a general meaning in the old Norse language. One is "ulcer," which is linked to gut feelings, passion, and following your dreams. The other meaning of the rune is the "torch," the symbol of enlightenment and transformation. It's believed to illuminate one's purpose or the need to follow your dreams regardless of outside influences.

X - Gebo

Gebo.
https://pixabay.com/es/illustrations/gebo-runa-runas-futhark-2644831/

Modern phoneme: G
English pronunciation: "GHEB-o"

In English, Gebo means "gift." However, this rune can also represent service, assistance, luck, or even partnerships you can obtain by providing the same. Gebo also illustrates the need for charity, generosity, and the exchange of equal-value properties. The appearance of the rune is also viewed as a sign of thankfulness.

ᛗ - Wunjo

Wunjo.
https://pixabay.com/es/illustrations/wunjo-runa-runas-futhark-2644556/

Modern phoneme: W
English pronunciation: "WOON-yo"

This rune represents joy, well-being, and happiness. However, Wunjo often signifies distress and challenges that predate the fulfillment of one's dreams. It can also signal impending changes and unexpected losses.

Heimdall's Aett

Heimdall is another powerful figure in Norse mythology. He is the gatekeeper and teacher of the deities. He is also the one who watches over the wisdom distributed by the gods. The runes of his aett lead the way to growth and prosperity. This is often obtained through a journey that contains both losses and successes.

H - Hagalaz

Hagalaz.
https://pixabay.com/es/illustrations/hagalaz-runa-runas-futhark-2644694/

Modern phoneme: H
English pronunciation: "HA-ga-lah"

Hagalaz means "hail" in English. This rune illustrates delay and difficulty releasing plans and the signal for change that's needed to move forward with your life. It's also linked to natural disasters and their consequences or unclear forces.

ᚾ - Naudhiz

Modern phoneme: N
English pronunciation: "NOWD-heez"

Naudhiz is the rune representing need in general. However, it may also signify difficulties, distress, the lack of a crucial quality, and resistance to change. The rune may also show that you will overcome life's hurdles by manifesting your wishes through intuitive practices.

I - Isa

Isa.
https://pixabay.com/es/illustrations/isa-runa-runas-futhark-adivinaci%c3%b3n-2644662/

Modern phoneme: I
English pronunciation: "EE-sa"

This rune signifies "ice," or being frozen in time, which means waiting. It also represents stillness, inertia, and the period of calm before taking action. It often appears as a period before a significant change, such as switching the course of your life, opening to a new perspective, etc.

ᛃ - Jera

Jera.
https://pixabay.com/es/illustrations/jera-runa-runas-futhark-2644821/

Modern phoneme: J / Y
English pronunciation: "YARE-a"

Jera, or "year" in English, is the old Norse symbol for harvest. However, the rune also means reaping your rewards for hard work or a successful conclusion of a difficult period. Jera can also showcase the beginning of a new life period cycle, the opportunity to grow and gather wisdom.

ᛇ - Eihwaz

Eihwaz.
https://pixabay.com/es/illustrations/eihwaz-runa-runas-futhark-2644633/

Modern phoneme: E / I
English pronunciation: "AY-wahz"

In the English language, this rune means "yew." In Norse lore, the yew tree symbolizes mystery and inspiration. It is believed to represent the stability and grounding needed to find spiritual wisdom. The rune can also show the sacrifices you need to make to thrive.

ᛈ - Perthro

Perthro.
https://pixabay.com/es/illustrations/perthro-runa-runas-futhark-2644941/

Modern phoneme: P
English pronunciation: "PER-thro"

Perthro is the symbol that represents fate and prophecy, although it's also linked to mysticism and the occult. It may reveal the correlation between present action and future outcomes. It can also mean industriousness, awareness, and fertility in different aspects of life.

ᛉ - Algiz

Modern phoneme: Z
English pronunciation: "AL-geez"

This rune means "elk" in English. This animal is known for its courage and protective nature. Consequently, the rune illustrates the need to listen to your creative instincts and their ability to bring enlightenment, good luck, and spiritual wisdom.

ᛋ - Sowilo

Sowilo.
https://pixabay.com/es/illustrations/sowilo-runa-runas-futhark-2644331/

Modern phoneme: S
English pronunciation: "So-WEE-lo"

Sowilo is the symbol of "sun" and happiness. Like its namesake, the rune also represents vitality, abundance in nourishment, and perseverance against challenges. Sowilo may also illuminate the path to finding solace, motivation, and true happiness in life.

Tyr's Aett

Tyr, the Norse deity ruling the skies, is also the symbol of war and justice. The runes in his aett refer to both physical and spiritual development. They also indicate that if you can focus on overcoming life's challenges, you'll be able to create a life of which you're proud.

↑ - Tiwaz
Modern phoneme: T
English pronunciation: "TEE-wahz"

The first rule in this aett is the most common symbol of "the god Thor." It symbolizes all the qualities he is feared and honored for, including strength, bravery, leadership, and honor. Tiwaz also appears to signify the greater good and sacrifices that lead to success.

ᛒ - Berkano

Berkano.
https://pixabay.com/es/illustrations/berkana-runa-runas-futhark-2644529/

Modern phoneme: B
English pronunciation: "BER-Kah-no"

Berkano is the Norse symbol for the birch tree, but it is also associated with the birch goddess. It represents the beginning of something new, rebirth, a period of fertility. It often appears in relationships, whether to signal to begin anew or to grow into something more powerful.

ᛗ - Ehwaz

Ehwaz.
https://pixabay.com/es/illustrations/ehwaz-runa-runas-futhark-2644896/

Modern phoneme: E
English pronunciation: "EH-wahz"

This rune means "horse" in modern English. As the Norse warriors' loyal companion, the horse is the ancient symbol of trust and partnership between different beings. It can also indicate fate in your success, instinctive behavior, and assistance.

ᛗ - Mannaz

Mannaz.
https://pixabay.com/es/illustrations/mannaz-runa-runas-futhark-2644241/

Modern phoneme: M
English pronunciation: "MAN-Naz"

Mannaz is the rune for the English word "man." It represents humanity and its qualities like mortality or going through the stages of life and death and forming communities where different values and skills can be developed.

ᛚ - Laguz

Laguz.
https://pixabay.com/es/illustrations/laguz-runa-runas-futhark-2644773/

Modern phoneme: L
English pronunciation: "LAH-gooz"

The meaning of this rune is tied to water, the unknown, potentials, the fluidity of emotions, and inner awareness of them. It also symbolizes open-mindedness, dreams, imagination, and emotional healing.

◊ - Ingwaz
Modern phoneme: Ng
English pronunciation: "ING-wahz"

This rune is linked to the god of Ingwaz. Like this deity, the rune presents sexuality, fresh energy, ancestors, family, wisdom accumulated over time, and spiritual growth. It also symbolizes a period of inner peace.

ᛟ - Othala

Othala.
https://pixabay.com/es/illustrations/othala-runa-runas-futhark-2644445/

Modern phoneme: O
English pronunciation: "OH-tha-la"

In English, this rune means "inheritance" or "tradition." Othala is linked to wisdom, property, and value that represent your legacy, the one you inherited from Others themselves. It can also represent homecoming, heritage, nobility, and talents.

ᛞ - Dagaz

Dagaz.
https://pixabay.com/es/illustrations/dagaz-runa-runas-futhark-2644493/

Modern phoneme: D
English pronunciation: "DAH-gahz"

Dagaz is a Norse word for "day." Just like a new day, this rune carries the meaning of hope, inspiration, awakening, and much-needed changes. It can also represent harmony, spiritual growth, clarity, self-awareness, and the ultimate happiness that comes with the realization of your dreams.

Runes in Practice

Besides magic, you can also use runes to translate short texts from English to Norse. For example, you can write your name or a simple phrase. It's a good idea to start with your name, as there are a few rules to writing in runes. Study the English equivalents of the runes from above before you start writing anything. Write them out on paper in the form of a table, so you'll have a reference anytime you need to look up a letter.

Remember to pen down the letters as you pronounce them. For example, if your name is Christina, you'll need to write "Kristina" in runes. In practice, this would look like this: ᚲᚱᛁᛋᛏᛁᚾᚨ.

Another rule of thumb is if you have a letter duplication in your name or the phrase you're trying to translate, these won't be duplicated in the Futhark. For instance, if your name is Emma, you'll write this as "Ema" in Futhark. In runes, this would look like this: ᛖᛗᚨ. The same rule applies if two consecutive letters correspond to the same rune. Let's say your name is Jack. The Kenaz rune corresponds to the letters "C" and "K," which means you'll have it twice in your name. However, you'll only write it once: ᛃᚨᚲ.

After writing down your first name, you can try to write your full name, including all last and middle names. When you're confident enough to write your full name correctly, you can move on to writing simple sentences. When you're writing more than one word or sentence, you can decide whether to leave a space between them or not. Some chose to use a dot (·) to separate the words, which is an easy way to ensure you're leaving enough space between the words. It also helps us remember which world each rule belongs to. Here are a few sentences to help you practice:

Today is a sunny day. ᛏᛟᛞᚨᛊ·ᛁᛊ·ᚨ·ᛊᚢᚾᛏᛊ·ᛞᚨᛊ

The cat is chasing its tail. ᚦᛖ·ᚲᚨᛏ·ᛁᛊ·ᚲᚺᚨᛊᛁᚷ·ᛁᛏᛊ·ᛏᚨᛁᛚ

I had a long walk, and I got tired. ᛁ·ᚺᚨᛞ·ᚨ·ᛚᛟᚷ·ᚹᚨᛚᚲ·ᚨᚾᛞ·ᛁ·ᚷᛟᛏ·ᛏᛁᚱᛖᛞ

Use your reference table to find the rune equivalent for the letters, write them out, then check if you got them right. Read back what you wrote to hear if it sounds right. Do this anytime you practice writing a word or sentence. Move on to a different word only after you are confident writing and reading the current one.

Meditation

To master runic divination, you'll need to connect with the energy of the runes. Meditation is a great way to get a sense of their energy and see which runes you might be drawn to and why. The symbolism related to the runes will be discussed in the next chapter, allowing you to discover more about why you may feel aligned with a specific rune. However, before you get to this part, you should spend a little time with the runes each day. That way, you'll be able to expand an understanding of their meanings from a conscious to an intuitive level, which you'll use in divination and magic. Learning the shapes of each rune, which aett they belong to, their English names, and symbolism before you start meditating with them is a good idea.

Choose a tranquil area where you won't be disturbed and prepare your body and mind for meditation. Wear comfortable clothes, and remove anything you might find constricting (including shoes, watch, jewelry, etc.). Sit in a relaxed position and take a few deep breaths to clear your mind from your daily preoccupations so that you can focus on the runes. Take a rune from your rune bag or box, and look at it for a few seconds. After this, close your eyes and imagine the rune standing tall in front of you. If you have trouble visualizing the runes this way, keep your eyes open and draw the shape of the rune with your hand in the air. Whichever method you choose, hold the rune in front of you and mentally retrace its outline.

Don't focus consciously on the meaning of the rune in front of you. Keep your attention on the rune's shape and concentrate on your intention of bonding with the rune. If your mind starts to wander, bring it back to the rune. Try to sense whether the rune is speaking to you and what the rune means to you in the present moment. Continue this for 15-30 minutes or until you can focus on this task. Repeat the following day with another rune until you go through them all.

Chapter 9: Runic Divination and Magic

Runes can be used for much more than just writing. This chapter will delve into how the runes were used for divination and other magical acts, including protection, assistance in spiritual growth, and much more. You'll also learn how Norse runes can be used for these purposes in modern times and what it takes to successfully master runic divination or magic.

Runes can be used for much more than just writing.
https://www.pexels.com/photo/runic-letters-on-wood-chunks-and-ground-with-autumn-leaves-10110445/

Using Runes for Divination

According to the ancient Norse people, the runes held many secrets, including information about the future. This belief came from the myth in which Odin himself uses the runes to prophesize. The term "rune" comes from an Old English translation of an ancient Norse word, which means "secret." This also hints at the mystical nature of the runes. Originally the runes were small staves with the letters of the futhark inscribed into them. The staves were made from the branches of a nut-bearing tree and later from wood, stone, or bones. These were cast during a small, or more often, elaborate ritual, where the rune caster sought information about the future. The prophet offered a quick prayer to the gods, looked up towards the sky, and cast the runes on a white cloth in front of them. Then, they interpreted the results by relying on their vast knowledge and experience in runic symbolism.

Making Your Own Rune Kit

Nowadays, you can buy pre-made runes and entire rune-casting kits. The runes can be made from stone, wood, or even crystals. The latter carries different magical energy but can be infused with even more natural power. You can also make your own rune set. This would foster a stronger connection between your energy and the runes, making it easier for your intuition to pick up their meaning. It's also not very expensive, which is perfect for beginners, especially if you're just figuring out whether runic divination is the best fit for your needs.

Here are some ways to make your rune kit:

- **From wood:** Trees were known to have magical powers in Norse mythology, so making runes from wood is a great option to ensure that you're starting off with powerful tools. Branches of living trees are the best due to the high concentration of their essence. Make sure you ask the tree permission before cutting it and give thanks after you're done. You can paint the runes on the wood, but you can also carve them into the wood as a more durable option.
- **From stones:** If you're living near a beach or river, you'll find flat pebbles or rocks that are the perfect size for runes. These

are more challenging to carve, but you can also paint the runes onto them and go over them with a clear protective coat to ensure that the inscription won't wear off too quickly.

- **From clay:** The most manageable material to work with, but make sure to bake the clay staves properly. Otherwise, they'll easily chip and crack. Coat these as well after baking.

When you've chosen your material, make 24 runes to account for the 24 letters of the Elder Futhark. Some people make a blank rune too, but it's up to you to decide whether or not you want one. You can also make a couple of extra ones, just in case you make an error during painting and carving. Make sure that all the staves are similar in size and shape and that they are no bigger than what would comfortably fit in the palm of your hand. Then, you can move on to inscribing the runes by focusing your intention on the name of each one while you're creating them. When painting, you should ideally use red coloring. This resembles the color of blood, the substance the ancient Norse traditionally used to paint runes.

Consecrating Your Runes

After creating them, you'll need to consecrate your runes. This will help you connect with them before using them for divination. To do this, you'll need a strong focus, so ensure you aren't too preoccupied with other things. There are many consecration rituals for runes and other magical tools, but here is a simple one suitable for beginners:

- Place the runes in front of you and a candle beside them on your altar or table.
- Light the candle and focus on its flame while you take a few deep breaths to help you focus.
- Take a rune into your hands, recite its name aloud and start moving it over the flame.
- Lay the rune down apart from the rest, and repeat with the remaining symbols.
- When you're finished, put the runes in a protective bag or box to keep them away from negative influences until you need to use them.

Casting the Runes

There are many ways to cast and interpret the runes for divination. While the previous chapter has introduced several meanings for each rune, the symbolic meaning during a prophecy depends entirely on your interpretation. For example, Isa means "ice," which can be interpreted as being stuck. However, when it comes up, you'll need to wonder whether you feel stuck or not. Maybe your gut is telling you that you have to stop and wait for a better opportunity. If this is your first thought when looking at Isa, it's probably the correct meaning for you at the time. Don't second guess your intuition; listen to it.

You can choose to follow the ancient method and toss the runes on a cloth to interpret them. You can also use one of the modern methods, which involves laying out the runes in a specific pattern, similar to the Tarot card layouts. Practice interpreting one rune at a time by asking questions that can be answered with a "Yes" or "No." These will only confirm what you already know in your subconscious but will help you get the hang of listening to your intuition.

Once you've mastered reading one rune, you can move on to a three-rune spread. For this, you'll need to take a deep breath, take out three runes, and lay them in front of you in a horizontal line. The middle one reflects your current situation and actions, and the one on the left shows past influences. While the rune on the right illustrates the most likely future outcome of your present actions. Another layout, the four-rune cast, is very similar to this one. The only difference is that you'll lay out the runes in a circular pattern and have an additional rune indicating other people's influence on your future.

When you've become confident in casting and interpreting simple spreads, you can move on to the 5, 7, 9, or even 24-rune spreads. The latter uses all 24 runes to give you a full scope of the events you can expect in the coming year.

The Five-Rune Layout

- After relaxing, lay out the runes in the shape of a cross.
- The rune at the base of the cross indicates general influences regarding the answer to your question.
- The rune at the left arm of the cross showcases the negative

forces affecting your future.
- The rune at the highest position alludes to the positive effects of current actions on future events.
- The rune at the right arm of the cross provides the most direct resolution to your inquiry or issue.
- The central rune represents future actions that will impact the answer to your inquiry.

The Spread of Seven Runes

- After clearing your mind with a deep breath, lay out seven runes in a V shape.
- The rune in the uppermost position on the left side indicates past events that can affect future outcomes.
- The next rune on the left represents the influence of your current actions or situation over future events.
- The last rune on the left side illuminates future behavior or events that may impact the answer to the inquiry.
- The rune at the base of the V tells you what to do to obtain the desired outcome.
- The first rune on the other side at the base of the V points to feelings that may impact your behavior.
- The rune above it shows hindrances and problems related to the inquiry.
- The last rune remaining indicates the most likely future developments associated with your inquiry.

A Simple Nine-Rune Cast

- Draw a deep breath and take nine runes from your rune bag or box while focusing on your question.
- Place the runes into your dominant hand.
- Closing your eyes, scatter the runes in front of you. Don't worry about how they land.
- Open your eyes and look at how the runes have landed.

- How many runes are facing up, and how many have landed face down? The ones facing up are influences you were already aware of and are likely interested in. The ones that landed face down are influences you weren't aware of.
- The runes that land close to the center represent the most significant influences you need to focus on. The ones towards the edge may have a lesser impact but shouldn't be disregarded either.

Using Runes for Magic

Other magical uses for runes included protection, love spells, talismans and charms, and bind runes. The latter involves combining two runes by writing and binding them together, letting them enhance each other's power. While these were less popular in ancient times, they are often used for different runic magic work in modern times. You can use them as sigils, amulets, or to enrich your spells and ask the deities for empowerment.

Here are some of the ways you can make bind runes:

- **Linear:** The runes are placed in the same line and used for several purposes.
- **Stacked:** The runes are placed onto the same axis, often used to represent reality.
- **Same stave:** Several runes are placed in a specific order along the same axis, used to eliminate a significant issue.
- **Radial:** Several runes share the same center point, perfect for defense magic as the runes are centering each other's power.

Runic spells, charms, and incantations were much more commonly used by the ancient Norse, and many are still in use today. These could be simple words, where one word has such a powerful effect that in itself is enough to take effect. An example of this would be the word "all," which has been found on amulets alongside Norse people's remains and was said to ward off evil spirits. Composite words were also used for inscriptions on charms, spells, and amulets. These were often used in elaborate rituals for fertility, protection, and summoning arches.

Sometimes complete spells were inscribed in the runic alphabet. One of these was the spells in which Odin was called upon to help find a thief:

"I call on you, Odin, the mightiest of gods.
Tell me the name of the person who stole from me.
Tell me now, who is taunting me so brazenly.
Show me, Odin. I call on you now.
I ask you to give the name of whoever stole.
And I thank you for your help."

Creating Your Own Charms and Spells

While you can use pre-existing charms and spells, creating your own would make them even more powerful. However, to do this, you'll need to understand how the position of the runes will impact their effectiveness in a charm or spell. Here are the positions to consider:

- **Direct position:** This works just like when a person stands directly in front of you so you can see their clear stance. This position of the runes indicates their most indicative values and symbolism. Use them to get straight to the point with your spell or charm.

- **Inverted runes:** These runes are influenced by a power that makes them behave differently. These are still related to the direct meaning of the runes but in a somewhat exaggerated version. They can come in handy when you need lots of power in your spell or charm.

- **Mirror position:** These runes are more powerful as they are created by other runes in the Elder Futhark. You can use them to make bind runes, but exercise precaution. If used incorrectly, they have the power to trap energy and provide very little in return. Some runes don't have a mirrored version, and these only are used for selfless actions.

Making your own spells and charms isn't the easiest task, especially if you're a novice. You'll need to work on your visualization technique and sharpen your intuition as much as possible. When creating a spell using runes, you'll need to visualize your intent, so it becomes a word you can see in front of you. The easier it is for you to do this, the more powerful your spell will be. An exercise that can help you learn how to visualize runes is simply picking one out from a table in front of you and trying to imagine it with your eyes closed. When you've mastered imagining the runes' shape, you can add textures or images to their forms. Try finding images that best represent their core meaning, and focus on these when trying to visualize them. This will help you memorize the details you'll need when trying to create the runes that best describe your intention.

Bind Runes

Forming bind runes will also require you to understand the essence of each individual rune. Some runes, when combined, develop a hidden meaning, which can affect the outcome of your spell or charm. Start practicing with a two-rune combination first, and make sure to have a short-term goal in mind while doing so. Analyze the two runes separately, consider their meaning, and contemplate what you want to achieve. Visualize your goals, and see if the runes will fit the purpose. If not, feel free to select runes with a meaning that's more aligned with your intention. Take your time with this step because some runes have multiple meanings.

Grab a pen and a piece of paper, and draw several combinations of the runes you've chosen. Don't worry about getting things right on the first try or even the tenth one. Just create whatever combination comes to your mind. When you think you have sufficient combinations, leave them for a while. Go finish an errand, or simply go for a walk. Sometimes the choice of the perfect rune will come to your mind while you're not focusing on it. If not, look at the sketches again and tap into your intuition to see which one you feel drawn to the most.

Next, depending on your purpose, select the material. If you have a long-term goal, you'll need something sturdy, like stone or wood. If you have a short-term goal, paper will also suffice. Don't forget to consider whether you want to create a spell, a talisman, or something else. For example, if you're making a protective charm for yourself, you'll need to carry it around to take effect. In this case, you can create a pendant for a necklace. However, if you need protection for your home, an art piece to hang on your walls would be a more suitable choice.

Carve or paint the bind rune in a calming atmosphere. You can meditate beforehand to relax your mind and let it focus on the task. You can repeat the meditation with your finished bind rune and thank your guides for their help. Keep the rune somewhere you can look at whenever you need to draw on its power.

Chapter 10: Galdr Magic

There are numerous misconceptions about the concept of Galdr. This false information is likely a result of how the practice was described in one of Edred Thorsson's books. The text suggested that it is the mere chanting of runes. Even though many people today practice Galdr this way, which is completely fine, it's not exactly how ancient Nordic people conducted this practice. That said, Galdr was primarily an oral tradition, which means that we have very little written evidence of this form of magic. After reading this chapter, you'll understand what Galdr is and learn about the history and origins of this magical practice. You'll also find out the uses of runes and Galdr and how to practice them. Finally, you'll come across a step-by-step guide on how to conduct the High-Seat Rite.

What Is Galdr?

Galdr is an Old Norse term from the Old English/High German word Galan, which means "singing incantations." The verb Galan means "to chant," and the Old English variation Galdor means "witchcraft/spell."

Galdr is a type of Norse magic that is practiced by chanting or singing incantations. There are two patron deities of this practice, Odin and Sigyn. Odin is the ruler of countless affairs, including magic and war. He is considered the patron of Galdr because he mastered 18 of these incantations. Sigyn is the goddess of victory and the wife of Loki. She is known for being the fetter or goddess of Galdr.

The History of Galdr

Before we get into the history of Galdr, we must first explore the idea of runes. While runes are the letters of the old Germanic alphabet, they are also defined as "incantations" or "symbols that carry a mystical or mysterious significance."

The term "rune" originated from Germanic languages and dialects and came from a verb that means "to whisper" and was then adopted by the Celtic alphabet as a term that means "secret."

This definition was then used to describe a hieroglyphic or ideographic symbol of a unit of mysterious lore, which served as a token for timeless concepts. Later, this symbol was adopted into another writing system which appointed a certain phonetic value to each hieroglyphic symbol. In modern times, people mistakenly describe runes as just letters of the alphabet.

Only a few forms of runes have been used to represent phonetic symbols throughout history. These could be referred to as letter runes. However, the majority's use remained for ideographic purposes - glyph runes.

Letter runes mainly developed and standardized within the magical futhark runic alphabetical system. That said, glyph runes also played a major role in the creation of Elder Futhark.

Magicians and priests during the Bronze Age, and even earlier, developed ideographic symbols that captured the essence of their magical and spiritual practices and teachings. Countless rocks in Scandinavia have carvings of these graphic expressions. These holy symbols, often referred to as pre-runic signs, gave rise to letter and glyph runes.

Pre-runic signs were purely ideographic until they came in contact with Mediterranean cultures. Only then did Germanic peoples learn about the concept of symbolic representation of phonetics and language during around the 2nd century BCE.

Germanic peoples represented their phonetics with runes that somewhat resemble Greek, Etruscan, or Latin characters. This idea is particularly relevant to the creation of galdrar and highlights the practice's significance to particular runic forms.

The initial stage of the development of the runic system served as the framework for rune magic. At that time, these ideographs weren't available for public use. They were incorporated into magical number formulas and sounds, or galdrar, and were used to induce certain magical results. Soon after that, runes were publicly used to express the written forms of the Germanic language.

It should be noted that magical connotations were only minimal during these stages of runic development. However, all three ideographic, phonetic, and sound-formulaic runic formulations were used together and can all be incorporated into modern-day runic practices.

The Uses of Runes and Galdr

Runes can be incorporated into magical practices in a plethora of ways. However, in ancient times, talismanic magic was perhaps the most common rune magic method. This method requires practitioners to carve runes into numerous objects before imbuing them with psychic power. Doing so was thought to induce changes in the magician, or vitki, and their environment.

In the 44th chapter of the Egils Saga, which is a saga about Egill Skallagrímsson's clan, Egill worries that someone is trying to kill him by poisoning his drink. He inscribed runes on the horn that contained the drink and stabbed his hand to color the runes with blood. This causes the horn to shatter to release all the poison. Hundreds of runic talismans remain to this day and can be examined to gain a deeper understanding of the magic behind them.

There are generally two types of galdr - poetic runagaldrar, which refers to magical runic incantations, and stadhagaldr, which means posture incantation or magic. Poetic runagaldrar was also commonly practiced. The Poetic Edda, which is an Old Norse collection of anonymous narrative poems, uses the voice of several of these ancient runic magical incantations. The drinking horns of Gallehus serve as evidence for stadhagaldr. These drinking horns have several magical formulas inscribed on them. Many of them portray human-like figures standing in runic postures. It is believed that children were taught the alphabet by using stadhagaldr methods. They had children stand in poses that resembled each letter.

The Galdr is the basic form of a mantra or incantation. You can think of it as the rune's vibratory expression. Galdr is an indispensable tool to the vitki throughout all the phases of rune magic. It is the medium that allows the runic force to manifest itself. The Galdr formulae are highly adaptable and can be flexibly incorporated into several practices. This is why each practitioner must experiment with it. The simple sound Galdr, which we will be exploring in more depth, is the most basic and practical when it comes to conducting self-guided ritual work.

Methods of Practice

If you're conducting basic magic while working with runes, you can either use Galdr or Taufr. Like Galdr, a Taufr can be described as a talisman or incantation.

There are no existing records of how the ancient Norse practiced Galdr, but there are two popular ways to practice this art according to modern practices. Edred Thorsson mentions one of them in his book, where he explains that you can recite the Elder Futhark runes in the form of a sing-song. Doing so would help you raise your vibrational frequencies to meet the vibrations of the runes. Thorsson's method was believed to be inspired by Guido von Liszt, who sought out the chanting technique from Hindu practices. Hindus believe that certain words possess a unique set of attributes. When you put them together, you will come up with mantras that induce unique effects. Those Hindu chants are known as seed mantras.

Guido von Liszt made up his own version of this practice and applied it to Armanen runes. Bringing vowels and consonants together allows you to create a Galdr, which, like a seed mantra, generates a specific desired effect. Thorsson expanded on this concept by applying it to Elder Futhark. You can chant the combination of Futhark rune vowels and consonants to generate the Galdr.

If you wish to try out the other method, you would have to write up a poetic spell. This spell must make use of the symbolic meanings of the runes. You should also employ poetic devices in the process. These devices are mainly alliteration and kennings. After the spell is formulated, it is sung to generate the Galdr.

There isn't much that we know regarding the Taufr, except that it is a talisman that was inscribed into various materials found in nature.

Magical practices were thought to be centered around it. The Taufr draws its power from the runes that are on it. The runes also determine the purpose of the Taufr.

Practicing Galdr

There were both male and female practitioners of Galdr. This was one of the very few Norse magical practices that people didn't call men who practiced it "unmanly." Surprisingly, some people considered it a manly form of magic. However, women who practiced it weren't considered any less feminine.

Since we don't have much evidence on how runes were historically incorporated into the practice of Galdr, it's fine if you wish to try your own take on the practice. Some incantations were completed in the Galdralag poetic meter, which was created for spells. While these incantations were more formal, informal methods were also used. Evidence suggests that Galdr was mainly based on creative wording and poetic language. It represents the intrinsic power of words.

Galdr was used in many instances. For instance, practitioners were thought to be able to induce storms, cast madness onto a person, cause faraway ships to sink, ease the process of childbirth, soften armor, decide which side emerges victorious in battle, and turn swords blunt.

Several poems in the Poetic Edda, such as Hávamál, reference Galdr. It was widely believed that Odin knew 18 Galdrar against numerous forces. The Edda also explained that the deity could bring the deceased to life.

The Galdralag Poetic Meter

Evidence suggests that Galdralag was only used for magical incantations. While most poetry today focuses on rhyming, Old Norse poetry emphasized alliteration, which commonly included tongue twisters. Alliteration is the repetition of sounds at the start of words. Ancient Norse poetry also focused on the use of kennings, which are similar to metaphors. Complex kennings are often very hard to grasp.

Ljoðaháttr, which is the poetic meter of chants, and Galdralag are much alike. While the former is composed of a total of six lines, Galdralag contains seven lines. Ljoðaháttr includes a line that is paired with alliteration, followed by a line that's unpaired. This means that lines 1 and 2 and 4 and 5 are paired, while 3 and 6 are unpaired. A Galdralag follows the same structure, in addition to a 7th unpaired line, which emphasizes the one before it.

You only need one alliterated word in each of the paired lines in Galdralag. However, it's fine if you wish to add more. The unpaired lines must have at least two alliterated words each.

Many practitioners frown upon the modern version of Galdr, which was created by Edred Thorsson, because it only requires you to repeat the name of the Futhark. They suggest that it lacks any substance and may even be disrespectful to the original, ancient practice. While some of their arguments make sense, we believe that the modern version of Galdr is an acceptable form of practice.

This table only includes the first 4 futhark names to give you an insight into their symbolic meanings and the phonetic values that they represent:

Name	Phonetic Value	Symbol
Fehu	F	Mobile force, energy, power, fertility, destruction, creation
Uruz	U, V	Health, strength, organic organization, wealth
Thurisaz	Th	Power of defense and destruction, action, the regeneration that follows destruction, applied power
Ansuz	A	Expression, transformation, ecstasy, inspiration, death mystery

High-Seat Rite: Step-By-Step Guide

This rite is one of the most common Norse rituals that combine divination and singing spells.

You'll Need the following:
- An offering
- A High Seat
- A cloak
- A drum
- A staff

Before you start, you will need to invite at least 8 people over to conduct the ritual with you, as these are the roles that you need to fill:

- **The Seer:** The person who travels to Helheim
- **The Master of Ceremonies**: The one responsible for directing the rite
- **The watcher/watchers**: The person or people observing the ritual
- **The battery:** The people responsible for raising the energy
- **The chorus**: The ones who sing and invite spirits over
- **The audience**: The ones responsible for asking the questions

You must also purify your space before conducting your ritual. In that case, you'll want to cast a protective circle and invoke the deity you wish to work with, Hel, Odin, or Freyja. You should always ask Hel permission to enter Helheim, as it's her realm. If you believe that the answer you received is "no," don't proceed with the rite under any circumstances.

If she grants you permission to enter Helheim, you should start building up the energy you need for your rite. Get everyone involved in the process, as raising the energy should be done through drumming and dancing ecstatically. Once you're done, sit and gather around in a circle and start calling on your ancestors and spirit to join you.

The Master of Ceremonies should ask everyone to visualize the world tree floating right in the middle of the space. They should also instruct everyone to chant Galdr and the Vardlokkur, which are protective chants that help you call on healing spirits and guardians beforehand. The whole group should be putting some physical input into the rite, whether they're clapping, moving, or influencing the rite in some other way. Up to this moment, all the work put into the rite is aimed at readying the Seer.

Once the Seer feels like they're well-prepared, they should take the cloak and staff. The Master of the Ceremonies should pay attention to the Seer, as they're the one who'll determine when it's time for the Seer to walk the path. Once everyone quietens down, the Master of the Ceremonies should guide the Seer through. They'll direct the Seer via visualization and ask them to imagine themselves in a field surrounded by soft soil. The Seer should visualize himself sinking into the cool soil below their feet.

The Master of the Ceremonies should then physically guide the Seer to walk into a spiral. This spiral is symbolic of the Yggdrasil. Then, the Master of Ceremonies should guide the Seer, via visualization, through the path-walking experience as they travel to Helheim. They should then be guided to the High Chair, where they'll describe everything they see. The Master of Ceremonies should avoid calling the Seer by name as they guide them through the questions. Even though this is their role, addressing them by it will only break them from their trance state. When the Master of Ceremonies is done asking the questions, the Seer should leave Helheim and then be called by their name. This will bring them back. They should remove the cloak, and everyone should stop the music. The offerings should be provided before giving thanks to bring the rite to an end.

Now that you have read this chapter, you know everything you need about the history and uses of Galdr magic. While very little is known about how this form of magic was practiced among ancient Norse peoples, you can still explore the modern renditions of the practice.

Conclusion

The concepts of Norse mythology that have been passed down to us are quite misleading and even nuanced in some ways. The sources of these stories and history are countless, and many of them paint very different pictures of Viking history and mythology. While these sources have provided us with a range of information concerning the Norse world, its beliefs, and the stories of the otherworld, there are considerable pieces missing and altered from these legendary tales.

We have an immensely vibrant and vivid image of the Norse culture, history, spirituality, and mythology, but we are far from understanding the full story. Unsurprisingly, considering how long it has been, there is no course that we can take to fill these gaps. Understandably, many people who deem Norse and Viking history and spirituality important have tried to fill these missing pieces with two approaches.

They undertake heaps of literature and scholarly research to understand how the history played out and what the origin stories of Norse mythology were. This method definitely produces more esteemed and credible sources of information. However, the unavailability of sufficient literature is a serious obstacle to this approach. An alternative solution to the problem of missing information is through creative imagination. Many authors use this method to create stories and assume historical events through imagination and mere common sense.

Plus, contrary to what many people think, there's nothing actually methodologically wrong with this approach unless you're writing for an audience that demands an extreme level of thoroughness when it comes to research. After all, that's what the Vikings themselves used to do. In fact, many authors back then did the exact same thing. Why do you imagine we have so many variations in the telling of these stories? It's because the people who were narrating these stories in the past constantly added new elements to these tales.

Many would add, subtract, and alter the happenings in these myths and even in actual history. Ultimately, this is how living traditions are passed down from generation to generation. They're not fossils that need to be mindlessly passed over the same way again and again. They constantly change and evolve with time and norms. After all, no tradition can live on without a little alteration and innovation.

As such, Norse history, culture and mythology were thoroughly infused with this view, and people today are fully aware of this. However, it does not lessen their interest in the subject. If anything, it makes their thirst for knowledge even more. If you're one of these people, hopefully, the contents of this book have quenched your thirst for knowledge regarding Norse traditions, culture, religion, and mythology.

If you're still buzzing with questions, a whole world of information is available for you online. Ultimately, Norse culture and mythology are a rich part of history. The gods were pillars who held everything together by tirelessly defending and fighting for this world. This attitude was adopted by the Viking races so unflinchingly strong. All this left an abundance of stories and myths for you to learn from.

Glossary: Norse Terms

Aesir

This is the classification of Gods mentioned in Scandinavian culture or Norse mythology. They were warrior deities who resided in Asgard. They were in opposition to Vanir, who were considered to be older deities associated with earth. Though there are varied mentions of Aesir deities in literature, this list usually includes Odin, Freya, Thor, Loki, Tui, Balder, Vali, Odinir, Brag, and Hoenir.

Altar

A designated flat space exclusively used for worship, magical practice, and religious customs.

Asatru

The contemporary reestablishment of Germanic paganism is dedicated to the old deities of Norse mythology.

Ax

The Ax holds a special meaning in Norse symbolism. It was not just a common weapon used by the Vikings but also considered a holy sign.

Balder

The son of Odin, and Freya, Balder was one of the purest Aesir deities. His mother made everything in the world swear an oath not to harm him, except for mistletoe. The trickster god Loki used this exception to kill him.

Balefire
A special fire lit for magical practices or traditional festivals like Beltane, Yule, Samhain, or Midsummer.

Berserker
Considered to be a legendary Norse champion, Berserker was known for his savage and reckless nature during battle.

Bifrost
The inter-cosmic bridge connecting different realms to Asgard. It is usually depicted as a giant rainbow bridge. It is mainly said to connect Asgard and Midgard.

Blot
A sacrifice or offering presented to the Gods or other deities common in Germanic Paganism and Neopaganism. This offering is usually in the form of a feast.

Cauldron
A large pot in spell work and rituals in Norse magic practices. Cauldrons represent the Goddess and water of rebirth.

Centering
The process of grounding your energy before rituals. This is usually done through meditation or other similar techniques.

Casting Circle
A casting circle refers to an area of sacred space that has been consecrated for use in worship. This space is typically referred to as a "ring of stones," and it is typically used by practitioners of the Norse religion or heathenism. Casting circles have deep roots in Norse culture and tradition, with many examples of these sacred spaces left throughout Northern Europe. One of the most commonly-known examples comes from the island of Öland in Sweden, where archaeologists have discovered more than 80 rings dating back thousands of years.

Cleansing
The process of eliminating negative energy from an object or surrounding space.

Dis
A spirit or deity associated with fate or fertility. These spirits can be both benevolent and spiteful toward humans.

Divination
The art of gathering information from the collective unconsciousness or universal guides. The process can be aided with the help of divination tools and techniques.

Dwarf
Mythical creatures that are skilled in metalwork and mining.

Elf
A supernatural being mentioned in many myths and stories. Elves are delicate, magical creatures with pointy ears.

Esbat
A Norse ritual that takes place during a full moon.

Fylgja
According to Norse mythology, Fylgia is a magical creature that accompanies people. This creature usually appears in the form of an animal and is believed to be a true reflection of the person's character or soul.

Galdr
The Norse word for incantation or spell. This was usually practiced in combination with rituals by both men and women.

Grounding
The process of dispelling any extra energy produced after a magical ritual by dissipating it into the earth. This process is also done to center oneself before a ritual.

Hammer
The hammer is not just a tool used in Norse culture but is also a representation. It is the symbol of Thor and a tool that can be used to create and destroy. Hammer charms were often worn for protection.

Havamal
A renowned poem that is included in the great Poetic Edda. The Poetic Edda is a collection of many Norse poems dating all the way back to the ancient Norse civilization. Havamal itself is a collection of different poems combined together.

Hel

Hel is the underworld of Norse mythology and the name of the Goddess who ruled it. Writers often use the name Hela so that the two won't be confused. According to some legends, Hela was the daughter of Loki, the trickster God. Some myths claim that she was rotting flesh and nothing else from the waist down. Hel, the underworld, was just as dreadful. It was a place where the people who died from sickness would go.

Herbalism

The art of utilizing herbs and plants to heal and treat diseases. It was a very prevalent technique in Norse history.

Jotunn

Roughly translated to giant, the Jotunn in Norse mythology are a race of spirits of nature who have superhuman powers. Legend suggests that they usually stand in opposition to the Aesir and Vanir.

Libation

The offering is presented to a deity, spirit, or ghost as part of a ritual.

Loki

The mischievous trickster god, Loki, was often confused as the God of evil. Norse mythology depicts him as the father of Hela and Fenrir. According to older legends, Loki planned Balder's death, for which he was punished by being bound to a rock until Ragnarök, a major event in Norse mythology.

Mead

A famous drink in Norse mythology, mead is a combination of fermented honey and water. It was usually served in Valhalla to the warriors after they had had a long day of fighting and training.

Norns

The Norns were the three virgin goddesses of fate and destiny; they were said to sit beneath the tree of life and spin the webs of destiny.

Oath

A formal promise or agreement, usually through invoking a divine entity as a witness, regarding one's intentions or future behavior.

Odin

The major God in Norse mythology, Odin, is a famous deity known by almost everyone. He was the inspiration for many famous poems in Norse history.

Poetic Edda

A very famous collection of pre-historic poems from the Norse age. It is one of the primary sources of Norse mythology.

Runes

Ancient letters used by Norse people. They were used for various purposes, including writing, magic rituals, and divination. People who didn't have writing systems saw the runes themselves as magic.

Runecasting

Rune casting is a divination technique used to obtain guidance from your subconscious mind. While many people argue that the source of guidance is divine, it's actually your subconscious mind guiding you toward the correct choice.

Sabbat

The eight Wiccan celebrations are meant to celebrate seasonal transitions. These include Imbolc, Ostara, Beltane, Litha, Lughnasadh, Mabon, Samhain, and Yule.

Seidr

The ancient term for sorcery was practiced back in the late Scandinavian iron age in Norse society. Many scholars and historians have argued over the nature of this practice. They ultimately agreed that it was shamanic and involved visual journeys.

Skald

A word of ancient Norse culture, it roughly translates to *poet*. It was used to refer to a court poet or bard from the ninth century onwards. Skald was a reciter and composer of legendary poems paying tribute to the brave heroes and their deeds. The accomplishment of being a successful composer was regarded as highly as being a warrior.

Spell

A magical practice that is non-religious in nature. It is done by speaking words, chanting, and gesturing. A spell should be clear, concise, and done with genuine intent.

Spirit

There are many meanings associated with the word spirit, but most of them relate it to a non-corporeal being. This word is also often used to refer to someone's personality, consciousness, or soul. Spirits can also be the surviving notion of a deceased person.

Stadhagaldr

A type of runic yoga famous in Norse history. The gestures and postures are similar to the magical form of the runes.

Sword

Another weapon commonly used in ancient Norse civilizations. The sword was a symbol of nobility and bravery. It was considered to be the embodiment of one's family legacy.

Talisman

A sacred object used to attract a specific kind of energy or force to its owner.

Teutonic

The ancient language of the Germanic Norse civilizations.

Troll

Another supernatural creature with a distinct appearance is mentioned frequently in Norse mythology. Trolls were either depicted as giants or dwarfs. They were said to live in small family units in caves or mountains.

Valhalla

Valhalla was the sacred place designated for fallen warriors who died heroically in battle. This place was depicted as a stunning palace of spears with a ceiling made out of shields. Considered to be presided over by Odin, Valhalla was the afterlife for brave warriors.

Valkyries

The Valkyries were the ones who took the fallen warriors into Valhalla. Their name translates to choosers of the slain. These beings were considered to be fate weavers and often took on the role of the Norse Norns.

Vanir

The Vanir were another group of deities in Norse mythology associated with fertility and nature. They were also associated with youth, luck, health, and magic.

Völva

A powerful seer and prophetess, Volva was a female magic practitioner in the ancient Norse society. She was able to foretell events of the future and provide warnings. According to a famous myth, Odin called Volva from the dead, only to have her tell him how the world would end.

Yggdrasil

Yggdrasil is also commonly known as the tree of life in many Norse legends. It has played a central role in many legendary stories. According to one legend, the nine realms came into existence around this mythical tree.

Here's another book by Silvia Hill that you might like

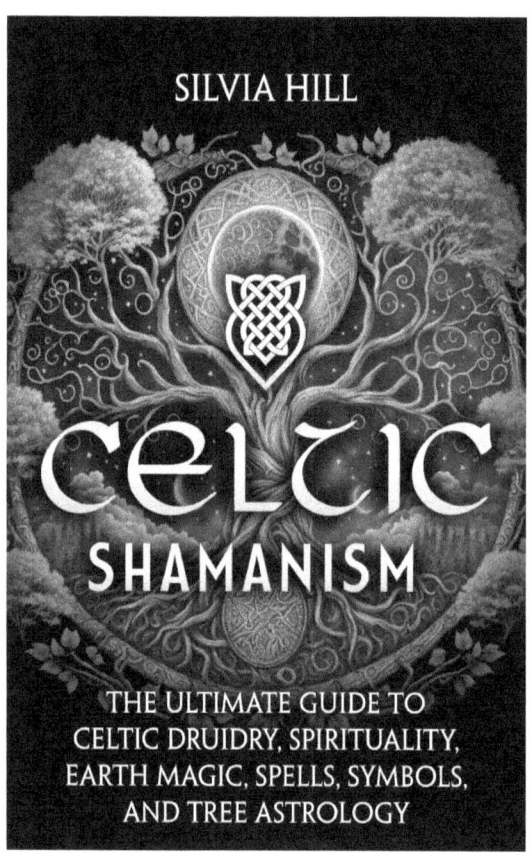

Free Bonus from Silvia Hill available for limited time

Hi Spirituality Lovers!

My name is Silvia Hill, and first off, I want to THANK YOU for reading my book.

Now you have a chance to join my exclusive spirituality email list so you can get the ebooks below for free as well as the potential to get more spirituality ebooks for free! Simply click the link below to join.

P.S. Remember that it's 100% free to join the list.

~~$27~~ **FREE BONUSES**

- 9 Types of Spirit Guides and How to Connect to Them
- How to Develop Your Intuition: 7 Secrets for Psychic Development and Tarot Reading
- Tarot Reading Secrets for Love, Career, and General Messages

Access your free bonuses here
https://livetolearn.lpages.co/norse-spirituality-paperback/

References

Nomads, T. (2022, March 21). Norse paganism for beginners: Quick introduction + resources. Time Nomads | Your Pagan Store Online. https://www.timenomads.com/norse-paganism-for-beginners/

A guide to Norse gods and goddesses - center of excellence. (2018, October 29). Centreofexcellence.com. https://www.centreofexcellence.com/norse-gods-goddesses/

About: Norse cosmology. (n.d.). DBpedia. https://dbpedia.org/page/Norse_cosmology

Apel, T. (2020a, August 2). Freya. Mythopedia. https://mythopedia.com/topics/freya

Apel, T. (2020b, August 3). Loki. Mythopedia. https://mythopedia.com/topics/loki

Apel, T. (2020c, August 3). Thor. Mythopedia. https://mythopedia.com/topics/thor

Christensen, C. (2020, October 8). This is why Odin sacrificed his eye in Norse mythology. Scandinavia Facts. https://scandinaviafacts.com/this-is-why-odin-sacrificed-his-eye/

Cruz, C. (2018, March 16). Yggdrasil, the Norse world tree. Tales by Trees. https://www.talesbytrees.com/yggdrasil-the-norse-world-tree/

Dan. (2012a, November 14). Cosmology. Norse Mythology for Smart People. https://norse-mythology.org/cosmology/

Dan. (2012b, November 15). Mimir. Norse Mythology for Smart People. https://norse-mythology.org/gods-and-creatures/others/mimir/

Dan. (2012c, November 15). Niflheim. Norse Mythology for Smart People. https://norse-mythology.org/cosmology/the-nine-worlds/niflheim/

Dan. (2012d, November 15). The Aesir-Vanir War. Norse Mythology for Smart People. https://norse-mythology.org/tales/the-aesir-vanir-war/

Dan. (2012e, November 15). Yggdrasil. Norse Mythology for Smart People. https://norse-mythology.org/cosmology/yggdrasil-and-the-well-of-urd/

Mark, J. J. (2018). Nine realms of Norse cosmology. World History Encyclopedia. https://www.worldhistory.org/article/1305/nine-realms-of-norse-cosmology/

Norse cosmology. (2021, May 12). Mythopedia. https://mythopedia.com/topics/norse-cosmology

Scott, J. (2020, December 3). A beginner's guide to Norse mythology. Life in Norway. https://www.lifeinnorway.net/norse-mythology/

Seven of the most important gods and goddesses in Norse mythology. (n.d.). Sky HISTORY TV Channel. https://www.history.co.uk/articles/seven-of-the-most-important-gods-and-goddesses-in-norse-mythology

The Editors of Encyclopedia Britannica. (2022). Odin. In Encyclopedia Britannica.

The mythological world of the Vikings. (n.d.). Historiska.Se. https://historiska.se/norse-mythology/mythological-world-of-the-vikings/

Apel, T. (2020, August 3). Fólkvangr. Mythopedia. https://mythopedia.com/topics/folkvangr

Dan. (2012a, November 14). Ancestors. Norse Mythology for Smart People. https://norse-mythology.org/gods-and-creatures/ancestors/

Dan. (2012b, November 14). Valkyries. Norse Mythology for Smart People. https://norse-mythology.org/gods-and-creatures/valkyries/

Dan. (2012c, November 15). Death and the Afterlife. Norse Mythology for Smart People. https://norse-mythology.org/concepts/death-and-the-afterlife/

Dan. (2012d, November 15). Hel (The Underworld). Norse Mythology for Smart People. https://norse-mythology.org/cosmology/the-nine-worlds/helheim/

Dan. (2012e, November 15). Valhalla. Norse Mythology for Smart People. https://norse-mythology.org/cosmology/valhalla/

Debutify. (n.d.). The Death and The Afterlife in Norse Mythology. VikingsBrandTM. https://www.vikingsbrand.co/blogs/norse-news/the-death-and-the-afterlife-in-norse-mythology

DK Find Out! (n.d.). DK Find Out! https://www.dkfindout.com/us/history/vikings/viking-warriors/

Mark, J. J. (2018). Norse ghosts & the afterlife. World History Encyclopedia. https://www.worldhistory.org/article/1290/norse-ghosts--the-afterlife/

Morgan, T. (2017, July 20). How did the Vikings honor their dead? HISTORY. https://www.history.com/news/how-did-the-vikings-honor-their-dead

Sogani, G. (2022, September 15). The idea of death and Hel in Norse mythos. Wondrium Daily. https://www.wondriumdaily.com/the-idea-of-death-and-hel-in-norse-mythos/

Tetrault, S., & BA. (2020, March 29). What's the Norse, or Viking, afterlife supposed to be like? Joincake.com. https://www.joincake.com/blog/norse-afterlife/

What can a Patronus say about a character? (2018, July 26). Wizardingworld.com; Wizarding World Digital. https://www.wizardingworld.com/features/what-can-a-patronus-say-about-a-character

Ásatrú and heathenry, belief and beards, racists and reporters. (n.d.). Norsemyth.org. https://www.norsemyth.org/2019/01/asatru-and-heathenry-belief-and-beards.html

Blain, J., & Wallis, R. J. (2009). Heathenry. In Handbook of Contemporary Paganism (pp. 413–432). BRILL.

Dan. (2012, November 15). Shamanism. Norse Mythology for Smart People. https://norse-mythology.org/concepts/shamanism

arithharger. (2015, September 4). Norse Shamanism. Whispers of Yggdrasil. https://arithharger.wordpress.com/2015/09/04/norse-shamanism/

The Return of the Völva: Recovering the Practice of Seiðr. (2012, February 15). Seidh.Org. https://seidh.org/articles/seidh/

Dan. (2012, November 15). Seidr. Norse Mythology for Smart People. https://norse-mythology.org/concepts/seidr/

Silver. (n.d.). Nordic Wiccan. Blogspot.Com. http://nordicwiccan.blogspot.com/2014/10/seidr.html

Circle-casting basics: All you need to know about magick circles. (n.d.). Grove and Grotto. https://www.groveandgrotto.com/blogs/articles/circle-casting-basics-all-you-need-to-know-about-magick-circles

Silver. (n.d.). Nordic Wiccan. Blogspot.Com. http://nordicwiccan.blogspot.com/2014/08/circle.html

Høst, A. [UCfgfjfS3huQ5mtaaZhsZDAg]. (2022, April 13). SEIDR 7:8 - The Craft in Seiðr. Youtube. https://www.youtube.com/watch?v=yF3H6xbWKkI

Høst, A. [UCfgfjfS3huQ5mtaaZhsZDAg]. (2022, April 27). SEIDR 8:8 - Planting our Staff in our own Turf. Youtube. https://www.youtube.com/watch?v=DuXF4Djc0kc&list=TLPQMTUxMDIwMjJg9ubefND5Ng&index=1

Dan. (2012a, November 14). The Vanir Gods and Goddesses. Norse Mythology for Smart People. https://norse-mythology.org/gods-and-creatures/the-vanir-gods-and-goddesses/

Dan. (2012b, November 15). Freyja. Norse Mythology for Smart People.

Dan. (2012c, November 15). Shamanism. Norse Mythology for Smart People. https://norse-mythology.org/concepts/shamanism/

Dan. (2014, November 3). Odr (god). Norse Mythology for Smart People. https://norse-mythology.org/odr-god/

Dowdeswell, M. (2022, September 17). The story, symbols and powers of Freyja, the Norse goddess of love. Ancient Origins

Freyja the goddess of love in Norse mythology. (n.d.). Bartleby.com. https://www.bartleby.com/essay/Freyja-The-Goddess-Of-Love-In-Norse-PCJEXC76JG

Inner Tapestry. (2018, October 17). Seiðstafr: The Norse shaman's staff of power. The HeartGlow Center. https://www.heartglowcenter.com/post/sei%C3%B0stafr-the-norse-shaman-s-staff-of-power

Norse shamanism: A Völva and her prophecies were feared among Norse gods and Vikings. (2020, May 19). Ancient Pages. https://www.ancientpages.com/2020/05/19/norse-shamanism-volva-prophecies-feared-among-norse-gods-vikings/

The return of the völva: Recovering the practice of seiðr. (2012, February 15). Seidh.org. https://seidh.org/articles/seidh/

Útiseta: The Norse shaman's wilderness quest. (2016, May 16). Shamamabear's Blog. https://shamamabear.wordpress.com/2016/05/16/utiseta-the-norse-shamans-wilderness-quest/

Viking archaeology. (n.d.). Archeurope.Info. http://viking.archeurope.info/index.php?page=seidr

Winquist, A. (2020, May 14). Meditation for protection with goddess Freyja —. The Soul Institute for Quantum Living.

Liam. (2022, January 23). Yggdrasil. Norse Mythology & Viking History. https://vikingr.org/norse-cosmology/yggdrasil-world-tree

Yggdrasil: The sacred ash tree of Norse mythology. (n.d.). The Public Domain Review https://publicdomainreview.org/collection/yggdrasil-the-sacred-ash-tree-of-norse-mythology

Dan. (2012, November 15). Ragnarok. Norse Mythology for Smart People. https://norse-mythology.org/tales/ragnarok/

Rhys, D. (2020, August 5). Yggdrasil symbol – origins and meaning. Symbol Sage. https://symbolsage.com/yggdrasil-symbol-meaning/

HeritageDaily. (2018, August 2). Yggdrasil and the 9 Norse worlds. HeritageDaily - Archaeology News; HeritageDaily. https://www.heritagedaily.com/2018/08/yggdrasil-and-the-9-norse-worlds/121244

Mark, J. J. (2018). Nine realms of Norse cosmology. World History Encyclopedia. https://www.worldhistory.org/article/1305/nine-realms-of-norse-cosmology/

www.ingramcontent.com/pod-product-compliance
Lightning Source LLC
Chambersburg PA
CBHW072105050526
44107CB00099B/533